The Soviet Perspective on the Strategic Defense Initiative

Dmitry Mikheyev

Foreign Policy Report
1987

A Publication of the
INSTITUTE FOR FOREIGN POLICY ANALYSIS, INC.
Cambridge, Massachusetts, and Washington, D.C.

PERGAMON·BRASSEY'S
International Defense Publishers
Washington New York Oxford Toronto Sydney Frankfurt

Pergamon Press Offices:

U.S.A. (Editorial)	Pergamon-Brassey's International Defense Publishers, 1340 Old Chain Bridge Road, McLean, Virginia 22101
(Orders & Inquiries)	Pergamon Press, Maxwell House, Fairview Park, Elmsford, New York 10523, U.S.A.
U.K. (Editorial)	Brassey's Defence Publishers, 24 Gray's Inn Road, London WC1X 8HR
(Orders & Enquiries)	Brassey's Defence Publishers, Headington Hill Hall, Oxford OX3 0BW, England
PEOPLE'S REPUBLIC OF CHINA	Pergamon Press, Qianmen Hotel, Beijing, People's Republic of China
FEDERAL REPUBLIC OF GERMANY	Pergamon Press, Hammerweg 6, D-6242 Kronberg, Federal Republic of Germany
BRAZIL	Pergamon Editora, Rua Eça de Queiros, 346, CEP 04011, São Paulo, Brazil
AUSTRALIA	Pergamon Press (Aust.) Pty., P.O. Box 544, Potts Point, NSW 2011, Australia
JAPAN	Pergamon Press, 8th Floor, Matsuoka Central Building, 1-7-1 Nishishinjuku, Shinjuku-ku, Tokyo 160, Japan
CANADA	Pergamon Press Canada, Suite 104, 150 Consumers Road, Willowdale, Ontario M2J 1P9, Canada

---

Library of Congress Cataloging-in-Publication Data

Mikheev, Dmitrii, 1941–
The Soviet perspective on the Strategic Defense Initiative.

(Foreign policy report)
1. Strategic Defense Initiative. 2. Soviet Union—Military policy. 3. Soviet Union—Military relations—United States. 4. United States—Military relations—Soviet Union. I. Title.
UG743.M55 1987 358'.1754'0947 87-2323
ISBN 0-08-035748-2

First Printing 1987

Printed by Corporate Press, Inc., Washington, D.C.

Contents

Preface v

Acknowledgements vii

Summary Overview ix

Introduction 1

1. The Soviet Mentality and the Party's Struggle 4

2. The Military and Ideological Consequences of SDI 26

3. The Technological and Economic Ramifications of SDI 48

4. Possible Soviet Responses to SDI 66

Conclusions 86

Preface

Even before the decision announced by President Reagan in his address of March 23, 1983, to press forward with a U.S. strategic defense research program, there was substantial interest in the United States in the role of strategic defense in Soviet military thought and in actual weapons policy. Even a cursory examination of the literature produced by the Soviet Union for use within its own policy structure reveals the importance ascribed to defensive capabilities, whose minimal purpose would be to afford protection to the Soviet military structure. Thus the Soviet opposition is directed not at the concept of strategic defense per se, but instead at the efforts of the United States to develop and eventually deploy such a system.

It is usually assumed that the Soviet motivation for a concerted campaign against the strategic defense program of the United States lies principally, if not exclusively, in military considerations. To be sure, as the author of this Foreign Policy Report suggests, the Soviet leadership seeks to deny to the United States a level of protection from strategic missiles that the Soviet Union itself would deploy for its own security. Indeed, the Soviet Union already possesses the world's only deployed ABM system. There is mounting evidence of the development by the Soviet Union of the components of an extensive strategic defense system, within which Moscow will "break out" of the ABM Treaty. Nevertheless, the analysis contained in this Foreign Policy Report is based upon a thesis that reveals a much broader Soviet motivation in opposing the strategic defense research program of the United States: its ultimate impact on the political system and socio-economic structure of the Soviet Union itself.

If the thesis developed in this work is correct, the stakes for the United States in the pursuit of strategic defense, including not only its military potential in effecting a new basis for deterrence of nuclear war but also for bringing about other spinoffs—economic and political—are far greater than have been envisaged. Therefore, it is timely and appropriate to make available this Foreign Policy Report as a contribution to the ongoing discussion of strategic defense and its future within and beyond the evolving national security policy of the United States. It represents part of a series of studies and publications on aspects of strategic defense prepared under the auspices of the Institute for Foreign Policy Analysis.

Robert L. Pfaltzgraff, Jr.
President
Institute for Foreign Policy Analysis

Acknowledgements

The idea that I might write this book was born in the mind of William Geimer, the President of the Jamestown Foundation and a dear friend, in the summer of 1985. He knew of my background in physics, my interest in technological development, and my research on the subject of the Soviet political mentality. It was his view that this combination of interests gave me a unique perspective from which to assess and present the genuine Soviet fears and concerns related to the Strategic Defense Initiative—as distinguished from what we are told by the Soviet Union's spokesmen. Two other gentlemen expressed enthusiasm about this idea: R. Daniel McMichael, Secretary of both the Sarah Scaife and Carthage Foundations; and Robert L. Pfaltzgraff, Jr., President of the Institute for Foreign Policy Analysis in Cambridge.

The moral, financial, and technical support of these gentlemen and the institutions they lead made possible the completion of this book in less than a year. Another piece of extraordinary luck made the book reality—my introduction, through Bill Geimer, to Todd Leventhal, who turned out to be an ideal editor of my English, and indispensible as an interlocutor on all the ideas contained herein.

To these remarkable gentlemen, whom I am now privileged to call my friends, I offer my deepest thanks.

Finally, I must acknowledge one other—my mother, an extraordinary Russian lady. It is to her that the work of these pages is dedicated.

Summary Overview

The determination of the United States to investigate the possibility of a strategic defense has infused significant and complex new elements into the U.S./Soviet relationship. The implications extend over a far broader horizon than simply the strategic-military relationship between these two nations. The Strategic Defense Initiative (SDI) holds the potential of initiating a process which, if carried to its logical conclusion, could lead to fundamental economic and political change within the Soviet Union.

Yet U.S. policymakers and observers are not given to seeing such broad significance in the SDI effort. Instead, SDI is evaluated in accordance with criteria related to deterrence and defense. These include, for example, the cost effectiveness ratio between offensive and defensive systems—to what extent and at what cost defensive systems could be deployed to counter the offensive capabilities of the Soviet Union. To consider SDI only in such a narrow military context neglects a far more important series of potential ramifications.

A vastly different culture and historical experience, together with a political structure based on fundamentally different premises, shape the Soviet approach to strategic defense in general and Moscow's reaction to the SDI program in particular. The presumption of legitimacy for the Communist Party of the Soviet Union is based on its claim to a superior socio-political economic relationship flowing from the dialectical nationalism of Marxist-Leninist ideology. To the extent that capitalist systems have proven superior in their ability to generate innovative technology and higher living standards, the legitimacy of Party leadership has been implicitly challenged.

SDI holds the potential to exacerbate the major contradictions that already beset the Soviet regime, and thus to have an all-encompassing impact on the U.S./Soviet relationship. The effect of a continuing U.S. commitment to the program would be to present the Kremlin with a difficult dilemma. In order to remain technologically, economically, and indeed politically competitive, the Soviet Union must provide the sort of incentives required to make its economy more efficient; to increase overall productivity; and to improve the quality and international competitiveness of its products. These incentives exist in the operation of a market mechanism; yet to adopt such measures would be tantamount to challenging the ideological credibility of the communist regime directly, and would render untenable its claim of socialism's "superiority." The Soviet Union could draw upon its vast technological and scientific potential; it could draw on its huge reserve of underutilized industrial capacity more effectively to compete in the international marketplace. However, each of these options carries a cost as well. Clearly, the adoption of the market mechanism could make a major contribution to the efficiency and strength of the Soviet economy. The attendant threat thus posed to the political leadership, however, makes this an unlikely course for the foreseeable future. In short, SDI places before Moscow the following problem: to survive, it must compete; to compete, it must reform; yet to reform is to admit the bankruptcy of the communist regime, and to make clear the unwisdom of totalitarian control.

Therefore, the Strategic Defense Initiative should be seen as the central element of a new U.S. global strategy, the goals of which might encompass:

- shifting from the "offense only" deterrence of mutual assured destruction (MAD) to a deterrent based more soundly on a mixture of offense and defense;
- significantly reducing the expansionism of the Soviet empire by reducing its internal capacity to sustain further external ventures;
- decreasing the degree of economic and political control exercised by Moscow over nations in the socialist orbit, particularly those in the Western Hemisphere and Eastern Europe;
- enhancing and broadening the conditions in which pluralistic societies and free institutions can flourish.

To such challenges the Soviet leaders find it necessary to respond in some fashion. The alternative is a loss of even that legitimacy which presently exists, together with the fear of losing hold of the reins of power. This response generally rests on the portrayal of all nations (particularly those of the industrialized West) outside the socialist orbit as "enemies of progress," "warmongers," "imperialists," or worse. In this way, the Party can maintain intact the mythology of struggle against enemies both without and within—a fundamentally important aspect of the Soviet political mentality. Moreover, Soviet leaders have historically succeeded in reinforcing the centrality of this perspective to political socialization by imposing a situation of "survival of the fittest" on the citizenry, through such means as forced collectivization and communal apartments.

Such is the broader context within which the Soviet response to SDI must be assessed. In the perspective of the Kremlin, the implications of SDI holding primary importance are those relating to its impact on the current and prospective military balance. On this plane, Soviet officialdom has forwarded a number of claims for public consumption as to the military purpose of SDI. In this view:

- The United States allegedly seeks through SDI the achievement of military superiority over the Soviet Union, hence threatening to disrupt the current strategic relationship of nuclear parity.
- SDI would undermine the arms control process (an American objective, it is held), and would moreover place the fate of humankind in the microcircuits of computers, not in human hands.

- Ultimately, hold the Soviets, the objective of a perfectly leakproof defensive shield will prove illusory; as such, there is no gain to be achieved by any such effort unless the ulterior objective is the militarization of space under U.S. domination. This, claim the Soviets, the United States seeks.
- In the near term, claim the Soviets, the United States seeks through SDI the acquisition of a first strike capability. The SDI program is held to furnish the potential for deploying the means to place at risk Soviet space assets and ground-based installations.

Each of these claims, upon closer examination, yields a certain mixture of truth and falsehood as a reflection of genuine Soviet concerns. Some are more accurate than others as a component of the Soviet view; each, however, answers a particular fear of the Soviet political mentality.

Seen from the Kremlin, SDI poses formidable technological and economic challenges to the Soviet Union. As the research program provides Western scientific applications both for an eventual strategic defense deployment and for spinoffs in the form of a wide variety of conventional applications, the gap between Soviet and Western technological capabilities will widen to Moscow's disadvantage. In this context, the importance of technological prowess as a guarantor of international prestige should not be overlooked. Moreover, a vast potential for improvement in the efficiency of production, the development of new products, and the enhanced quality of products lies in the ability of SDI to bring forth technologies of wide commercial application. The impact on the relative position of Western and Eastern economies promises to be great indeed. In order to keep pace with these developments, Soviet leaders must undertake to hasten their technological progress and increase the efficiency of their production facilities. Yet such steps could not but undermine the ideological legitimacy of the Party leadership and open the dreaded possibility of political reform.

Yet the Soviet Union is not without alternative responses. The characteristic drive of U.S. defense planners for technological perfection often leads them to abandon proven state-of-the-art systems in favor of newer and more advanced programs not yet deployable. Meanwhile, the Soviets do not scrap deployed systems based on existing technologies. As a result, they maintain a force structure which is extensive in quantity and adequate in quality. While pressing its own weapons development and deployment, the Kremlin attempts to constrain American efforts by the use of treaties—on which subject a better understanding of the Party's attitude might modify the importance placed by U.S. officials on "successful" outcomes to negotiation efforts.

As a result of SDI, certain changes may be anticipated in the Soviet Union. In the political realm, Moscow will likely adopt both an overt and covert approach—one designed to entice the West away from SDI, the other intended to weaken its determination and ability to pursue the program. Militarily, an effort will be made to call into question the ultimate effectiveness of any SDI-developed system. (Evidence of this ploy can already be seen in the recent Soviet announcement of the "simple measures" to be taken in Soviet offensive forces, which supposedly will negate the effect of any U.S. defensive system.) Over the long term, an effort will likely be made to increase greatly the Soviet Union's capabilities in computer technology and information processing. In the economic area, fundamental changes in the Soviet system are unlikely. Instead, Soviet leaders could be expected to exploit the room for maneuver they enjoy owing to their monopoly of control over the system, by adopting such measures as contractual work, additional incentives to the scientific community, and perhaps greater automation of production.

Ultimately, the United States faces a choice. If it continues with the SDI program, it will pose challenges of unprecedented scope to the Soviet leadership. If the program is abandoned, the inherent opportunity to confront the Soviet leadership with difficult choices will be lost—perhaps irrevocably. U.S. decisionmakers, it is suggested, must therefore continue their support of the program. Seen in proper perspective, SDI can provide U.S. policy with the tools needed to fashion a comprehensive strategy vis-a-vis the Soviet Union. Conversely, reductions in SDI—signifying a weakening of U.S. determination to follow through on the prospects of a defense-oriented deterrent—will send to Moscow the signal that the dilemma need not be confronted.

Introduction

Understanding the Soviet Union's foreign policy is an unsurpassed intellectual challenge, even for someone who has watched the Soviet Union for decades on different levels, and from both vantage points—inside and outside.

Virtually every bit of information coming from the Soviet Union, be it a word or deed, is accompanied by another which contradicts it. True, the Soviet Communist Party's program and actions, when considered in a long time span, show a remarkable consistency, suggesting the existence of an ultimate goal and a steady strategy. Both clearly point to a determination to achieve world domination through spreading the Communist sociopolitical system throughout the world. However, this explanation is not intellectually satisfactory for several reasons. It is very difficult to accept the notion that anybody today can seriously believe in Communist ideology—certainly not Soviet people. It is equally difficult to comprehend why any nation would want to shoulder the burden of world domination.

What, then, is the driving force and the constituency behind consistent Soviet expansionism? If there is none—if the whole question is about the aspiration of a small oligarchy to rule—then, again, how could such an ambition possibly be entertained in light of no support and obvious failures on virtually every front?

These questions are not, unfortunately, merely an exciting intellectual exercise. They are directly related to our national survival and, moreover, to the future of mankind. These questions have acquired a particular practical importance, inasmuch as President Reagan's Strategic Defense Initiative has become a centerpiece of Soviet-U.S. relationships.

What is the Soviet perspective on SDI, and what is likely to be the Soviet response to SDI?

First, the Soviet leadership's strong and negative reaction to SDI leaves no doubt, particularly after the Reykjavik summit, that it perceives SDI not as just another defense program, but as an initiative that will influence the fundamental political, economic, ideological, and military calculations of the Kremlin.

Dozens of Soviet officials, and three successive General Secretaries of the Communist Party of the USSR, have made hundreds of statements rejecting SDI. Why? To what extent do official Soviet statements represent the actual concerns and fears of the Soviet leadership? Is the Soviet leadership really concerned about the United States acquiring a first-strike nuclear capability, about "computers being placed in charge of mankind's fate," about the militarization of space, or an increase in the danger of accidental nuclear war? Is it rather that they do not want to participate in a new arms race, because of the need for modernization and reform in their economy? In order to compete with the United States in a new arms race, will the Soviet Union introduce market-oriented reforms—or choose to close its society further, initiate a heightened Cold War and tighten discipline? Furthermore, suppose one way or another they did modernize their economy—what is going to happen then? Will the Soviet Union double its production of offensive weapons, or consider a preemptive nuclear strike when the United States starts actual deployment of a ballistic missile defense (BMD)? Or will the Soviet leadership instead be ready to reduce offensive weapons dramatically, since they will become useless anyway?

These and many other related questions make up a mind-boggling problem for political analysts and decisionmakers. Yet we cannot ignore them; SDI obviously has long-term ramifications for the future of mankind. None of the traditional approaches of Western Sovietologists—neither "historic Russian imperialism," nor communist ideology, nor even realpolitik—provide satisfactory answers. Instead, a different approach is necessary, based on a concept of the Soviet political mentality.

The SDI issue is a classic example of two totally different political mentalities at work. While Americans have agonized about the pros and cons of SDI—considering its costs, its effect on the balance of forces, and taking into account likely Soviet responses—for the Soviet leadership SDI has been perceived from the very beginning as a truly *strategic, political* challenge. According to the Soviet political mentality, the Communist Party of the Soviet Union is in a state of permanent political struggle for survival. This struggle takes place both on the domestic and international fronts. The Party perceives itself as a unique, totally new form of organization, incompatible with the rest of the sociopolitical environment of mankind. Therefore, permanent coexistence is impossible—the communist system will either triumph or perish. In other words, it is not a desire to dominate the world which drives the Party; it is, more accurately, its desire to survive, which is believed to be possible only through the ultimate global dominance of its political structure.

Because this struggle is strictly political, everything that affects it is a matter of politics. Therefore, real Soviet concerns about SDI are also primarily political. In other words, the Party is not chiefly concerned that SDI would give the United States a "first-strike capability," or that it would lead to the militarization of space. The Soviets are not even primarily concerned with the effect that SDI would have on the military balance per se. They know, for example, that the United States would never launch a nuclear attack except in the most extreme circumstances, and that it is extremely unlikely that nuclear weapons will ever be used militarily in any significant way. Instead, the Party is mostly concerned about the political ramifications of the technological lag behind the West (which would only be exacerbated by an all-out qualitative arms race); the consequences of SDI for Moscow's ability to project power throughout the world; and ultimately, SDI's effect on the struggle between the two superpowers for world domination.

The type of missile defenses envisioned by President Reagan would require of the entire Soviet economy a technological effort totally unlike anything it has yet confronted. It is doubtful whether this could be achieved without making fundamental political changes in the Soviet system. Without decentralizing its economy and introducing market forces, the Soviet Union might not be able to develop the necessary spectrum of technologies and the improvement in the quality of its industrial production required by BMD systems. Even a massive infusion of Western technology would not help the Soviets much, because of the constantly increasing complexity of production methods.

Therefore, the Soviet leadership is facing a painful dilemma. If SDI proceeds, the Party might lose the new technological race—and the ability to carry on its political struggle under the umbrella of the nuclear threat. The alternative is to restructure radically the Soviet socioeconomic system, by unleashing market forces and giving up the Party's monopoly on the economy and information. Both scenarios involve grave political risks, fraught with the potential for ultimate political defeat. By presenting the Soviet leaders with the inevitable and unpalatable choice—falling behind technologically, or radically restructuring their political system—SDI could be the leading edge of an overall U.S. policy toward the Soviet Union, whether or not it is recognized as such by U.S. leaders.

The Soviet perception of SDI as the Grand Plan to Destroy the Socialist System derives not from the actual goals of the President's initiative, but from the nature of Soviet political mentality. Therefore, in order to understand the Soviet leadership's concerns and fears about SDI, one must understand this mentality. We have to understand why it perceives the world as divided into two sociopolitical camps, engaged in a mortal struggle for world domination; we have to know why it perceives a pyramidal, hierarchical, sociopolitical structure in the future community of states as the most natural and stable world order. These and other features of the Soviet political mentality can hardly be explained by the Russian imperial tradition or by communist ideology alone. They are the results of a sociopolitical environment which has created a world view shared by both the leaders and the overwhelming majority of the Soviet population.

In sum, the concept of an unending, mortal struggle for survival in a hostile environment is a key to understanding Soviet foreign policy. In turn, this and other basic perceptions of the Soviet leadership can be understood only within the context of the Soviet political mentality.

1.
The Soviet Mentality and the Party's Struggle

Among American political scientists and policymakers, one can distinguish two main approaches toward discerning the real intentions and capabilities of the Soviet leadership. Purely for the sake of convenience, they may be labeled the liberal and conservative approaches. Two distinctive philosophies and psychological predispositions underlie these tendencies. Yet neither provide an adequate understanding of the Soviet threat.

Liberals tend to downplay the aggressiveness of both the Soviet Union and the Soviet mentality. They believe that the messianic component of communist ideology is pure rhetoric, retained exclusively for internal consumption. Liberals point to chronically lagging Soviet technology and to Soviet economic problems, and insist on this basis that the West exaggerates the Soviet military threat.[1] Liberals point out, correctly, that the West invented the atomic and neutron bombs; multiple, independently-targetable warheads; cruise missiles, aircraft carriers, "smart rocks," and so on. They emphasize the traditional Russian preoccupation with border protection, and advocate an accommodating attitude toward the Soviets, with an emphasis on finding ways to achieve mutual understanding and reduce fears through negotiations and agreements. Among other things, liberals overlook the fact that the Soviets do not want us to understand them and do not wish our fear of them to be reduced.

The conservatives, on the other hand, take communist claims of ultimate victory very seriously. They point out, quite rightly, that the Soviets have never abandoned their long-standing goal of destroying capitalism. The conservatives, in general, tend to take ideological considerations more seriously than liberals. They also point to the enormous resources of the Soviet Union, the ability of the Communist Party to concentrate them at crucial moments, and the tireless expansion of the Communist Party's domain. The conservatives note that the Soviets were the first to develop ICBMs, the hydrogen bomb, methods of underwater missile launching, and the "cold" launch technique (permitting missile reloading and refiring). The conservatives tend to downplay, however, the inefficiency of the Soviet economy, the extent to which its resources are stretched, and the growing technological gap between East and West. They overlook the limitations of the Soviet

[1] The best and most recent example of this approach is a book by Tom Gervasi, *The Myth of Soviet Military Superiority* (New York: Harper and Row, 1986).

system and ignore how paranoid and frightened the Soviets are of the "imperialists' " might.

Understanding Soviet behavior has never been easy, especially for Westerners. The problem is even more complex now that the Soviet Union, having suffered serious economic and political setbacks, has nevertheless managed to evolve into a truly global power. The riddle can be resolved with the help of our concept of the Soviet political mentality, which encompasses communist ideology, Russian cultural traditions, and national character—its "Slavic soul." It embraces those constants that are shared by both the Soviet masses and their leaders, past and present. As Urie Bronfenbrenner wrote:

> Soviet behavior is determined by Soviet perceptions, Soviet fears, and Soviet modes of thought. Any attempt to predict how Russians would react, which is based solely on considerations of strategy, deductive reasoning, and assumptions (usually unrecognized) that their thought processes are similar to our own, is doomed to miss the mark.[2]

Mentality

Mentality—that is, a set of basic perceptions of time, the nature of the physical and social environment, the nature of life and human relations—combined with one's perception of potentials and goals, determines to a large degree the orientation of an individual in the socio-political environment. Mentality, as a set of perceptions and attitudes, makes up for missing pieces in the picture of environment in which socialization is to take place. It also serves to limit what solutions are considered plausible. As long as it is intuition, not logic, that leads the search for solutions to problems when information is incomplete, the direction taken in the search is determined primarily by our perceptions and attitudes—that is, by mentality. For example, an individual who sees the world as essentially hostile and dangerous will tend to exaggerate threats and underestimate promises in a new situation. Therefore, his approach will be cautious: one small step, a pause and one more step, and so on. Being constantly on guard against traps, an individual of this mentality needs more time for orientation. On the other hand, the area of his potential solutions will be much wider. In contrast, a "pyramidal mentality" will lead those possessing it to search for structure and hierarchy even if there is none, while a "pluralistic mentality" might ignore the existence of an obvious hierarchy and instead search for alternative centers of power or authority.

If perceptions of power and attitudes toward "proper" power sharing are added to the basic perceptions, the political mentality will be derived.

[2] Urie Bronfenbrenner, "Allowing for Soviet Perceptions," in Roger Fisher, editor, *International Conflict and Behavioral Science: The Craigville Papers* (New York: Basic Books, 1964), p. 168.

More than anything else it is this perspective, or mindset, which shapes political behavior in a society. Taking the process one step further—to the international plane—we have only to add one's perception of the international environment and of the nature of relations between states. Therefore, to answer the daunting questions of Soviet international behavior, and the impact of the Strategic Defense Initiative on it, the proper place to start is with an analysis of the Soviet mentality in general and the Soviet political mentality in particular. It is also important to delineate how the American mentality differs from that of the Soviet Union, and how, therefore, one can escape the trap of mirror-imaging.

Perceptions and Attitudes

Fundamental perceptions and attitudes are shaped during childhood in the process of our interaction with physical and social environments. The physical environment to which American and Soviet children must adapt differs considerably between the two countries. Although the environment varies significantly from place to place, we can safely say that, overall, an American child will encounter a physical environment warmer, lighter, softer, more colorful, brighter, faster, sweeter, bigger, and less crowded than that within which his Soviet counterpart develops. In general, life will be more demanding on the Soviet child than on the American one; it will require of him much more creativity and forcefulness, both in terms of adapting to and influencing the environment, and in strengthening his body. Thus, the Soviet child is much more likely to develop a high degree of physical tolerance and endurance.

The social environments in the Soviet Union and the United States are also distinct. Apart from several big metropolitan areas like New York, a typical social environment in the United States is far safer and friendlier—contrary to the popular belief about the absence of crime in the Soviet Union. Adversarial relationships permeate Soviet society on all levels: between "*vlasti*" (authorities) and "us," between children and grownups, between youngsters of one street or borough and another, between neighbors, between city dwellers and "hungry provincials," and so on. While American parents and psychologists are preoccupied with the problem of protecting American children from stress, Soviet boys have to learn how to fight with the help of stones, sticks, or at least fists, in order to survive.[3] Bravery is the most highly praised virtue among Soviet boys, while the reputation of being a coward can ruin one's life. (In the Soviet movie "Scarecrow," produced by Roland Bykov, the atmosphere of hostility, cruelty, and even sadism among Soviet teenagers was well portrayed. None of the many American movies

---

[3] See, for example, "Children Under Stress," *U.S. News and World Report*, October 27, 1986.

on the subject of teenage delinquency portray the almost delight-filled sadism which is displayed by ordinary Soviet schoolboys and girls.) Many close observers of the Soviet scene have pointed to the unusually high level of suspiciousness among the Soviet people themselves, to say nothing of their mistrust of foreigners. Examples of this are plentiful in literature about the Soviet Union. In one case, a Soviet writer says: "This distrust [toward other people] is inside us; it does not come from outside. It is older than Stalin, older than communism, maybe older than the czars."[4]

A small poll was conducted by the author among former Soviet citizens who were asked directly whether they thought man is basically good or evil. Sixty-two percent of the fifty-four persons polled said that man is basically evil; twenty-nine percent replied that the question was incorrect, or invalid, while only nine percent thought that man is basically good. This contrasts with a poll among roughly six hundred and fifty mostly white, young, urban middle-class Americans, of whom the same question was asked. Eighty-two percent believed that man is basically good, and only six percent responded that man is basically evil, roughly the exact opposite of the Soviet response. This informal poll was not scientific, but it would not be surprising if a more professional one replicated its findings.

These results are not surprising if we consider the impact of the social environment on a person's mentality. The social environment can be divided into relatively permanent and variable components, which may be respectively termed "social culture" and "social turmoils." The former suggests the normal, enduring strands of everyday life, which embrace traditions, mores, religious and sociopolitical values. These form the permanent matrix of a society. Social turmoils, on the other hand, are serious disturbances that are superimposed on the social culture. They include wars, revolutions, riots, deportations, arrests, famine, purges, and natural disasters which intrude upon normal life and have important sociopolitical consequences.

Although social culture affects every member of a society, social turmoils usually affect only part of the population. Even revolutions do not involve the entire population; they have their full impact only after they have transformed the social culture through a "cultural revolution" such as occurred in the Soviet Union during the 1930s and in China in the late 1960s and 1970s.

---

[4] Cited in Susan Jacoby, *Moscow Conversations* (New York: Coward, McCann & Geoghagan, 1972), p. 249. Geoffrey Gorer and John Rickman have written in their psychological study of the Russians: "This [Russian] fear would appear to take the form of an emotional conviction that there exists in the external world an enemy (or enemies) who plan to constrict and destroy them, but no sort of certainty concerning the identity of the enemy." Geoffrey Gorer and John Rickman, *The People of Great Russia, a Psychological Study* (London: The Cresset Press, 1949), p. 154.

Social Turmoils

From accounts of American Vietnam War veterans and the former hostages held in Iran, it is apparent that turmoils have an especially strong impact on those for whom such events are the exception rather than the rule. One is struck by the high rate of mental disturbance reported in these individuals, who were exposed to violent death, torture, or prolonged stress.[5] Given that one quarter of American Vietnam veterans have suffered some kind of emotional disorder, it might be a surprise to find any sane people at all among the wartime generations of Germans, Israelis, Russians, Vietnamese, or Lebanese. Perhaps the American psyche is more fragile than those of other nations. In any event, if a relatively short traumatic experience can seriously threaten a person's mental integrity, we can reasonably assume that prolonged and dramatic social turmoils involving almost the entire population of a country can radically transform a country's social culture and leave a significant imprint on its mentality.

America's social environment has been undergoing constant and fairly rapid change for several centuries. Yet, with the dramatic exception of the Civil War, these changes did not disrupt the society's fabric; rather, they shaped it in keeping with ongoing economic and technological development. It is true that immigrants, upon arriving in America, underwent dramatic personal experiences and cultural shock. This was usually for the better, however, and often occured at a mature age. Since, perhaps, the War of 1812, America's national security has never been seriously threatened, and the foreign wars in which it participated have never been of the total type, involving every member of its society. America's quite unique sense of security was graphically described by Abraham Lincoln in 1837 this way: "All the armies of Europe, Asia, and Africa combined, with all the treasure of the earth (our own excepted) in their military chest, with Bonaparte for a commander, could not by force take a drink from the Ohio . . . ." No other major nation in the world has had such a sense of security—amounting to a self-perception of near invulnerability. Certainly no other has enjoyed so long and uninterrupted a period of organic development in the direction of prosperity.

In contrast, the longest period of social tranquility in Russia during the first half of the twentieth century lasted only eight years, from 1906 to 1914. In consequence, the remainder of this period was one of almost uninterrupted social turmoil, affecting three full generations. Aside from a few brief interludes, the synopsis of social turmoil in Russia in the first half of the twentieth century is as follows:

[5] For example: "Vietnam veterans are 86% more likely to kill themselves than those who did not serve in Vietnam." From *The New England Journal of Medicine*, cited in "A Vietnam Vet's Suicide Pact," by Collen O'Connor and Shawn Doherty, *Newsweek*, March, 1986.

1904-1906	The 1905 Revolution and the Russo-Japanese War.
1914-1922	World War I, the October Revolution, the Civil War, and famine.
1928-1933	Collectivization and famine.
1936-1947	The purges, the Russo-Finnish War, World War II, famine, and the wars of resistance in the western Ukraine and the Baltic states.

Thus, we can safely assert that every citizen of the USSR over fifty years of age has lived through one of the most traumatic experiences known to mankind. One can hardly find a single person of this age group who has not killed someone, who was not a prisoner or a prison guard, who did not suffer starvation or see peasants dead of starvation on the outskirts of a big city, who did not deport peasants to Siberia, or was not dispossessed himself. Although the last thirty-six years present a striking contrast to the first half of the century, it should be remembered that the Soviet Union's current leaders grew up in the midst of this social turmoil. For them, the hardships were not an aberration but the normal social culture. We can see this in the example of Mikhail Gorbachev.

Gorbachev was two years old when, in the spring of 1933, people in his village eagerly awaited the appearance of the first grass—for food. He knows how precious food can be, and how it may be necessary to use all of one's powers to obtain it. He was six years old when people were disappearing during the night; in the morning, everybody was afraid even to ask their neighbors what had happened. He was eleven when the Nazis occupied his village and hanged several dozen communists and activists; he thus had a chance to see with his own eyes how fragile human life is, and how high status in the community can turn overnight into a great disadvantage. He was a teenager when he saw the land devastated by war, which would have imprinted upon him the fragility of the whole manmade environment. While a teenage boy, he probably participated in battles against boys of neighboring villages using stones, sticks, and perhaps knives. He was sixteen when a new famine came to his village, and when people were arrested for being prisoners of war or just for having lived under German occupation.

Under these circumstances, Mikhail Gorbachev grew up confronted by the seeming relativity of human values. He has experienced rapid change in the definition of who is a friend and who is the enemy, what is good and what is evil. He might have learned that the only reliable and unchanging point of reference in such circumstances is one's personal survival. By the end of this turbulent period in his nation's history, Gorbachev's mentality would have been fully formed. It is thus unlikely to have changed significantly during his climb to the uppermost levels of power in the Soviet system, even if his rise occurred during more prosperous periods.

Social Culture

As a result of the unprecedented social turmoils of the first half of the century, traditional Russian social culture underwent an important transformation and developed into a new form of culture, a "communal culture." Among its characteristics are communal apartments, public transportation, kindergartens, "pioneer camps," lines in stores and government offices, and other now-familiar features. Some of the most important elements of communal culture were present in the Russian peasant culture of the late nineteenth century. Unlike the farm laborers of Western Europe, Russian peasants were tightly clustered in villages and heavily dependent on the community. Since they were forced together involuntarily by a combination of the harsh physical environment and the law, Russian peasants did not accept other members of the community as their natural friends and brothers, except when they grouped together to face outsiders. They did not like the regimentation of communal living, and largely rejected it. For them it was never a community of love and partnership, as the Russian intelligentsia wanted to believe. The Russians did not relish close proximity—as the Japanese did, for example—nor did they have the opportunity to enjoy privacy, as did the Germans. In Russian, as in Japanese, there is no native word for "privacy." In general, the Russians felt comfortable with people around them only if they were the "right" people—that is, friends and (to a lesser extent) relatives.

These psychological aspects of peasant culture were transferred to the urbanized "communal culture" of Soviet cities. The most characteristic and fundamental feature of this culture is the communal apartment. When the "exploiting classes" were exterminated, several hundred thousand apartments in the cities became available to the millions of proletarians previously housed in slums or country villages. The change of lifestyle that this signified had a double effect. On the one hand, it meant an improvement in their physical environment, given the comparative safety and conveniences of such dwellings. But on the other hand, it had a harshening effect on their social environment. Each room in a house or apartment would typically be deemed sufficient for a whole family, usually consisting of between five and seven people, who would have to share all the basic amenities with all the other families under the same roof. One toilet, stove, bathroom, corridor, mailbox, and (later) telephone would be shared by thirty to forty people, generating cruel and fractious social conditions, day in and day out, for years.

Since competition for the staples of life is the rule of existence under these conditions, strength is naturally the most highly prized quality one can possess. Moreover, because one's own power—whether physical, financial, psychological or intellectual—cannot by itself provide sufficient security in such a crowded social environment, the support of others becomes a crucial necessity for survival. The community thus tends to fragment into numerous, mutually-supportive groups and subgroups: family members, friendly neighbors, peers, adults, personal friends, and so on. These groups are themselves in constant competition with each other, so that one learns to think in terms of "us vs. them" at a very early stage of socialization.

At the end of the 1950s the Party adopted a new housing policy, and the construction of apartments began on a mass scale. However, it took at least fifteen years before the number of families living in communal apartments was matched by the number living separate units. By then, two generations of Soviet citizens had passed through the institution of communal apartments. Only half of the children born after the end of the 1960s can claim to be escapees from the culture of communal apartments. They are now teenagers. They still do not have actual privacy, but they have less of a need to resort to the street in order to get away from the suffering inflicted by neighbors and family members. Hence, they are less prone to view neighbors as hostile competitors, having relegated them from the category of enemies to the category of neutrals.[6] Today, eighty percent of families in the Soviet Union live in separate apartments; therefore, eighty percent of all children born today will escape a key institution of communal culture.

Although communal apartments are slowly becoming a thing of the past, other elements of communal culture persist: fights at the bus stops in the morning, squabbles in lines for meat and vegetables in the evening, kindergartens, pioneer camps—and, of course, labor camps and the army. These last two institutions continue to mold about four million young Soviet men and women each year into tough, combative survivors. Virtually every male in the Soviet Union goes through at least one of these institutions, although the "education" is now somewhat shorter and less thorough than it was thirty years ago. This "softening" of the Soviet social culture could have been one of the reasons why the party decided to create a new school—the "Afghanistan School of Combatants."

Ethical Systems in the Soviet Union and the United States

As far as morality is concerned, the sociopolitical environment influences a maturing person through what we will label "channels of influence." In the United States, there are five major channels of influence: family, school,

---

[6] It is noteworthy that American attitudes toward neighbors differ radically. According to Geoffrey Gorer: ". . . each generation of Americans acquires in early childhood attitudes which will subsequently reinforce . . . the supreme importance of the neighbors as guides and exemplars." Geoffrey Gorer, *The American People, A Study in National Character* (New York: W. W. Norton & Company, 1964), p. 87.

church, the mass media, and the "street." The last category includes all the unorganized agents of influence: peers, neighbors, strangers, and so forth. All five channels of influence in the United States are independent; yet the messages of family, school, and church coincide considerably, leading to the formation of a "Super Code," a code based on religious ethics. Another code, the "Societal Code," is based on law. Finally, the "Functional Code" is the set of unwritten rules of daily conduct derived primarily from one's family, the mass media, and the "street." Although all three codes differ, in the United States they overlap considerably. For example, killing or lying is considered unacceptable by all three codes under virtually all circumstances.

In the Soviet Union, the situation is very different. There are only three main channels of influence: "School," a euphemism for all official institutions; the family; and the "street." The church and mass media for all practical purposes do not exist as independent channels of influence. The final result of the socialization process in the Soviet Union is the formation of two main codes of conduct: the "Societal Code"—that is, the official code—and the "Functional Code," the unwritten code of behavior. A "Super Code" based on absolute moral principles is practically nonexistent, and does not permeate the other two codes with its influence.

The peculiar nature of Soviet life derives from the fact that the Societal Code and Functional Code dictate for the most part different and often opposite rules of conduct. Stealing from the state, for example, is considered by the societal code a more serious offense than stealing from an individual. But the functional code does not even recognize stealing from the state as a crime, although it strongly condemns stealing from private individuals. Because these two codes hardly overlap, and because there is no "Super Code," morality in the Soviet Union is fundamentally relativistic: lying, cheating, and stealing by themselves have no positive or negative connotation. They have to be judged in terms of the particulars of the situation: they could be bad or good, depending on circumstances. One of the best expressions of this dichotomy was given by the adolescent daughters of a Soviet army officer: "In school they teach us one thing, and in the newspapers and books we read the same thing. But in life everything is quite different. Then is everything a lie? Do the newspapers lie, the teachers lie, the writers tell untruths?"[7] Virtually all Soviet children do eventually reach the conclusion that "everybody is lying." By the age of 12 and 13, as movie-maker Roland Bykov testifies, they learn to accept this dichotomy as the norm and do the same thing.[8]

---

[7] Klaus Mehnert, *Soviet Man and His World* (New York: Frederick A. Praeger, 1963), p. 221.

[8] Roland Bykov, *Eto Nashi Deti* (These Are Our Children), (Moscow: Avrora, 1984), a film.

Some Typical American Perceptions

A typical middle-class American perceives the physical environment as largely safe and friendly. The "zone of assured safety" for an American will embrace virtually the entire country, and many foreign lands as well. In other words, he would feel confident that he could count on finding food, clothing, and shelter in any part of the United States and in many other countries. A "gray area" would encompass most of the rest of the noncommunist world. The "dark area" would include very few countries.

An American will also perceive the social environment—with the exception of parts of several large metropolitan areas— as basically benign, if not friendly.[9] Partnership plays a more important role in his life than intimate friendship. In childhood, Americans are encouraged by their parents to look at life as essentially the pursuit of happiness, even if this pursuit is not always an easy task.[10] As a result, many young Americans perceive their goal in life as striving for happiness, and life itself as an exciting game. The perception of time held by a typical young American does not usually stretch far, either in the past or in the future; Americans live in the here and now.

The American perceives confrontation—and, especially, war—as an unfortunate disruption of normal life, which must be dealt with as quickly and efficiently as possible. He tends to avoid confrontation, and wants to be liked. He has difficulty in perceiving someone as a permanent or mortal enemy. The concept of indefinite struggle is completely alien to him. After he has "made his point," he prefers to help the defeated enemy in order to secure peace. The American perceives compromise as the essence of conflict resolution. He is usually ready to make reasonable concessions as a gesture of goodwill aimed at encouraging the other side to do the same. For him, a concession is an expression of self-confidence and goodwill, not a bribe intended to ensure good treatment. Diplomacy is essentially a search for a mutually beneficial accommodation through reciprocal compromises.

An ideal American group structure consists of partners. If a leader is necessary, his power should be controlled by the group through a variety of checks and balances. Americans perceive domination by one opinion or will as a threat to the opportunity to benefit from diversity; they will act strongly to prevent any domination.

---

[9] A typical American notion in this respect is presented by Ashley Montagu: "In recent years evidence has become available which indicates that human beings are born good—'good' in a sense that there is no evil or hostility in them, but that at birth they are wholly prepared, equipped, to function as creatures who not only want and need to be loved by others but who also want and need to love others." M. F. Ashley Montagu, *The Direction of Human Development, Biological and Social Bases* (New York, Harper and Brothers, 1955), p. 289.

[10] "There is this notion that everybody should be happy all the time," says psychologist Aletha Huston from the University of Kansas. ("Children Under Stress," ibid.)

The Model of the Soviet Mentality

Both the physical and social environments are perceived by the typical Soviet man as consisting of a relatively small "zone of assured safety," a somewhat bigger "zone of uncertainty," (the gray area), and very large "zone of danger," (the dark area). The physical environment outside the small "light area" is dangerous and life-threatening for at least six months of the year.

Man is seen as basically evil—that is, selfish, greedy, and cruel. He tends to take advantage of others, or to exploit them for personal gain, safety, and leisure. He is capable of good behavior only for fleeting moments, when overcome by the urge to sacrifice. Outside the very narrow circle of intimate friends and relatives, the social environment is dangerous; one has to be constantly on guard. Anarchy, when the evil in man is unleashed, represents the ultimate danger.

Life is seen as an incessant struggle for survival in competition with others for the scarce staples of life. Hence, a struggle for domination within a group is the most natural thing in the world; it is, in fact, the essence of human relations. Building a circle of intimate friends is extremely important in securing one's dominant position within a group. For the group to be able to act together coherently it must be carefully structured so that the most capable people occupy the upper layers in the pyramid, and are thus in a position to control and neutralize the selfish interests and evil intentions of all members. Justice is perceived as the equal distribution of both hardship and pleasure. If one wants more pleasure and less hardship, he must work to improve conditions for the group as a whole.[11]

Kindness, love, devotion, honesty, hatred, justice, and so on, are all perceived as relative values. Their worth is measured in terms of their usefulness in the struggle—that is, in terms of strength vs. weakness. In other words, they could be either helpful or detrimental to a person's survival, depending on circumstances. They should be used to maximize one's strengths and minimize one's weaknesses. Compromise is seen as a tactical maneuver, a temporary accommodation, which purpose is to appease the enemy when one is in a position of weakness. Accordingly, a concession is a kind of bribe intended to ensure good treatment.[12] Respect derives from the recognition of one's strength and bravery. Admitting to being scared is shameful and dangerous; bravery is seen as a manifestation of invulnerability. One seeks

[11] There are obvious inconsistencies in the way individuals perceive the "correct" group structure. On the one hand, the interests of the community are recognized to have priority over personal interests. On the other hand, one tends to think that his personal interests often fully coincide with those of the community.

[12] On the Soviet perception of compromise, see Vladimir Lefebre, *Algebra of Conscience* (Netherlands: Deidel, 1982), p. 6.

respect, not sympathy. In general, fear and hatred are considered to be more powerful and reliable forces than love and sympathy.

Government is seen as inevitably evil, but is preferred to the reign of unrestrained personal evil.[13] The law is the government's tool for restricting individual evil. Life is not necessarily perceived as progressively improving; it can improve or deteriorate. And although struggle is the very essence of life, war is a disaster. I't can (and must be) averted by skill, maneuver, long-term calculation, building the country's military might, and—ultimately—eliminating those who oppose you.

The Soviet Political Mentality

As long as politics revolves around the question of power, the political mentality of a nation can be derived from its basic perceptions considered together with the popular perception of power, its accumulation, maximization, and distribution within society or states. These latter two are directly related to the notion of a "right sociopolitical structure" of intersocial or international relations. Perhaps it is not surprising to say that the Soviet and American mentalities differ greatly toward power. The American mentality holds a much more positive perception of personal power than the Soviet one. The American perception of power allows not only the private possession of all forms of power—physical, economic, political, intellectual, spiritual (and even the power of arms)—but also a considerable concentration of it in private hands. Law and market forces stay on guard against overconcentration of one form of power, or the merger of different forms of it into one. This attitude toward personal power results from a trust in the positive overall balance of good and evil in man, as well as a recognition of the delicate balance that exists between creative and destructive power, and that the most difficult task is limiting the latter while simultaneously encouraging the former.

Marx, Lenin, and Attitudes Toward Power

Karl Marx was obviously troubled by the rise of a tremendously powerful class of capitalists, who managed to combine power over the people with the power of technology and thus epitomized the problem of overconcentration of the individual's power and its unequal distribution. The solution it offers to the question of power distribution is thought to be the most

[13] In the words of one of the shrewdest observers of Soviet Russia, Wright Miller: "External authority to the Russians, it would seem, has always been an evil to be tolerated only because of overriding necessity. . . ." Wright Miller, *Russians as People* (New York: E. P. Dutton & Company, 1961), p. 115.

important element of Marxism. Marx suggested that three major forms of power—military, economic, and political—should be taken from private hands and entrusted to an institution known as the "dictatorship of the proletariat." Behind this idea lies the pivotal notion that power can be good only if it belongs to everyone equally—that is, to no one in particular. Marx thought that by eliminating the individual's ability to accumulate power, the problems associated with it would eventually be entirely excluded from human relationships.

When Lenin, Trotsky, and their allies began the practical implementation of Marx's ideas, it soon became obvious to them that all forms of power are to some extent interchangeable. Intellectual power, for example, can be converted into financial power, and spiritual power can be easily turned into political power. In other words, the Leninists realized at the very beginning of their revolution that all forms of power had to be communized, if a small group of "professional revolutionaries" were to retain control over the whole nation for the indefinite future. At the beginning they even thought about taking from individuals their power over children, thus denying them the right of biological continuation.

Thus, the Bolsheviks brought the development of the Marx's ideas to their ultimate conclusion: all forms of power were to be communized, automatically making each one of them just another form of political power. Accordingly, it is not only war which is a continuation of politics by other means; in Lenin's interpretation of Clausewitz's famous maxim, *all* human activities are ultimately political. Science, the arts, sports—to say nothing of economics—all appeared to the Bolsheviks as, first and foremost, political activities. Marx's key "law" of social development as a struggle between classes for power was extended by the Bolsheviks to all forms of human activities. Everything became a struggle for power by different means. Moreover, every significant talent—being a source of potential influence—is considered by the communists a potential political power. Hence, every talent should be considered the "nation's property," and treated accordingly.

This is as true for the contemporary Soviet leadership as it was for the founding fathers of the first socialist state. For example, at the 24th Communist Party Congress in 1968, the Party stated:

> Today, when the class struggle between socialism and capitalism has sharpened dramatically, Soviet musicians are called upon to even more actively participate in the struggle against bourgeoisie ideology.

> It is a duty of every representative of the Soviet intelligentsia to repel any attack of bourgeoisie ideology, and to wage an active, offensive struggle against it. A

Soviet activist must be ideologically steadfast and uncompromising toward any form of alien influence.[14]

The communists' perception of power corresponds to the Soviet popular suspicion toward personal power. There is the widely spread belief that the power of individuals should be minimized and the power of the state maximized, because individuals can use it exclusively for their personal, egotistic purposes. There is also a popular belief that one's talent belongs to the nation—which leads to a genuine misunderstanding of the Western notion of talent as a commodity which can be sold.

These features of the Soviet mentality must be kept in mind when we think about possible changes in the Soviet sociopolitical system. Even very limited market-oriented reform would involve such questions as, for example, selling one's intellectual power or other talents on the market. This idea would require the considerable modification of popular Soviet beliefs; for, as they are held today, one cannot sell something that rightfully belongs to the state. It is noteworthy that those Western historians and political scientists who overemphasize the continuity between Tsarist absolutism and the communist totalitarianism of the Soviet Union tend to omit the fact that, despite all its absolutism, there was a considerable accumulation of power in private hands in prerevolutionary Russia. In contrast to the Soviet Union, this power was hereditary. Furthermore, although there was no separation of the Church and the state, the Church was a fairly independent actor with tremendous spiritual power, the guardian of an absolute moral code (the "Super Code").

Popular Sociopolitical Perceptions in the USSR

Political behavior in a society is usually a reflection of typical behavior in an elementary group, which is based on a set of basic perceptions about the environment, life, and power, along with one's perception of oneself, one's goals and capabilities. The notion of a "correct" distribution of power within an elementary group is, therefore, directly related to the notion of the "correct" social structure.[15] Not surprisingly, perhaps, the Soviet perception of the proper group structure differs drastically from that held by Americans.

As seen, the Soviet approach entails bitter competition, which may paralyze the group for an indefinite period. The members may thus sometimes opt for choosing a strong figure capable of terminating the struggle for the

[14] *Pravda*, December 17, 1968, and November 27, 1968.

[15] See Heinz Eulau, *The Behavioral Persuasion in Politics* (New York: Random House, 1967); and Harold D. Lasswell, *The Analysis of Political Behavior, An American Approach* (Great Britain: Anchor Books, 1966).

benefit of all. This process results in a pyramidal, hierarchical structure: the leader, his closest supporters, and the masses. In the competition for dominance, the contenders for power do their best to conceal any evil intentions or proclivities they may have. Thus, those who emerge as the actual leaders of the group are more likely to be characterized by domineering, authoritarian traits than by intelligence or superior capability. Once the structuring of the group is complete and a center of power is firmly established, the restructuring of the pyramid becomes almost impossible.

While to the American mentality a democratically-structured group or society may be more appealing—because it embodies tolerance, compromise, the dispersal of power, and partnership—the pyramidal structure has its own appeal to the Soviet mind. It restrains the destructive forces of competition after the initial struggle for dominance has been concluded; brings order; and promotes harmony, stability and the supremacy of social goals over personal ones. In other words, individual ambitions are kept under control, while the constructive potential of each individual serve the goals of the group. In the eyes of people of pyramidal mentality, democracy is only a transitional stage of the struggle for dominance.

In the Soviet mentality, a pyramidal, hierarchical social structure is appropriate not only for groups; it is also the model for society as a whole. In order to optimize its power, the nation should eliminate inner frictions and contradictions; therefore, it should be structured as one united body, with a brain, bones, muscles, circulatory and nervous systems. In other words, every form of power should be taken from individuals and private institutions, put together and transferred into one or another part of the nation's collective body. Thus, the intellectual capabilities and talents of the citizens form the brain of the nation; means of production are the skeleton. The military and police are the muscles, and so on. Ideally, all of them are supposed to work harmoniously and serve the interests of the nation as a whole.

This notion of a correct sociopolitical structure of the nation is such an important part of the Soviet mentality that even political opponents of the communist regime can hardly imagine "dismantling" the nation's heavy industry or creating a multiparty political system. These perceptions have even been incorporated into contemporary Soviet language, where one can now find such expressions as "planning organs," "party organs," and simply "the organs,"—a euphemism for the KGB and police.

Soviet Perceptions of the International Environment

The notion of a proper structure for society has application in the international realm as well. In the Soviet political mentality, the community of nations is in a state of bitter competition for a better place in what ultimately will be a united, global order encompassing all mankind. In other words, nations are struggling for survival, and use all means available to them: military, economic, cultural, religious, diplomatic, and so on. Eventually, humanity's "organism" will evolve a brain, bone structure, nervous and circulatory system, and all the vital organs. Only then will the struggle for power which characterizes current international relations cease, and a peaceful, harmonious life be achieved. In the race for the top position in the developing pyramid of mankind, only two contenders remain. Each one of them represents totally different sociopolitical systems and cultures. When one of them wins, therefore, the other will perish.

In the last decade or two, this popularly-held Soviet belief seems to have changed somewhat. Numerous domestic and international failures, the rise of China, the accumulation of nuclear weapons, and other factors have led some people to favor an accommodation between the United States and the Soviet Union, so that the world will be divided into two spheres of influence ruled by the mutual consent of the superpowers. This idea seems to have a number of supporters among the Soviet military and certainly among the intelligentsia.[16]

The Party's Claim to Leadership

The Communist Party of the Soviet Union leaves no doubt that it aspires to be the brain of a future integrated structure of mankind. After all, its Central Committee is the brain of the party, which is the "vanguard of the proletariat"—which, in turn, is the "vanguard of the Soviet people," which are the vanguard of the "working people of the world," which constitutes the very body of mankind. From the Party's point of view, it alone is best positioned and equipped to organize all of humanity. It will certainly not be the anarchic forces of capitalism—pulling in opposite directions, determined by parochial and egotistic interests—which finally bring together the myriad cultures and political structures of the world. As Leonid Brezhnev put it in 1977:

> The Communist Party is the vanguard of the Soviet people, their most conscious and progressive section, inseparably united with the people as a whole. The party has no other interests at heart but the interests of the people. To try to counterpose

[16] Two very revealing articles on this subject are: T. Savchenko, "*Sovetskie Ofitsery*" (Soviet Officers), *Veche*, No. 12, 1984; and Alexander Vasiliev, "*Real'naya Ideologia Praviashchego Sloya*" (Real Ideology of the Ruling Layer) *Posev*, No. 9, 1986).

the party to the people by talking about the "dictatorship of the party" is tantamount to trying to separate, say, the heart from the whole of the body.[17]

A Popular View on the Party's Leadership

Today, there are many reasons to believe that people of the Soviet Union are questioning every point in Brezhnev's statement. They do not see Party members as the most conscious and progressive sector of Soviet society. They think that the Party has indeed separated itself from the body of the nation; they believe that Party members have all interests but the interests of the people at heart. Many of them feel that the country is under the Party's thumb. Above all, it is a widely accepted belief that the Party is the most corrupt part of the society—so much so that many people feel nostalgic for Stalin. They are so angry at the corruption of the Party elite that they tend to forget the fact that Stalin's terror was directed as much at the masses as it was aimed at elements in the Party.

In sum, the Soviet people are not prepared to dismantle or reconsider their pyramidal mentality, yet they are ready to embrace some other mechanism for upscale movement within the pyramid. The Party, for its part, is well aware of the popular view. For several years now it has promoted the idea that it is capable of rejuvenation; that it can invigorate and cleanse itself; and that there is no alternative to it.

The "Struggle" of the Party

The Party's reaction to SDI, and the actions it has taken in response, must be considered in context of the Party's overall struggle. Only within the framework of the Party's political struggle can one comprehend the place and role allocated in it to the military in general, and to the strategic nuclear forces in particular.

It is often said that American leaders play poker, while the Soviets leaders play chess. Unfortunately, in the international arena, the Soviets do not play games, neither chess nor Russian roulette. Instead, they are waging a mortal struggle, one infinitely more complex, dangerous, and rewarding than a game. American military strategists have an odd infatuation with the theory of war developed by Carl von Clauzewitz. Perhaps this is because Clauzewitz's teaching so closely reminds one of chess. The communists, however, took Sun Tzu's writings on war, assimilated Napoleon's and Clauzewitz's concepts of total war, took advantage of newest technological means of controlling

[17] *Pravda*, October 5, 1977.

the masses, and created a strategy of protracted struggle—which fits perfectly their political mentality.

No matter how we may feel about the Communist Party, we cannot deny it credit for developing a formidable strategy of total struggle against an overwhelmingly stronger enemy. After all, this strategy has been carried out with phenomenal success. Starting with a handful of people in a backward country, the Party has waged its struggle against the entire world—including its own people—for almost ninety years, and has done remarkably well. In the words of Leonid Brezhnev:

> We were the first. We did not have an easy time. We had to hold out in a hostile encirclement. We had to break out of age-old backwardness. We had to surmount the enormous force of historical inertia and learn to live by new laws of collectivism. Today, when we assess the main result of six decades of struggle and work, we can say with pride: We have held our ground; we have stood fast and won.[18]

Brezhnev's claim of victory might be somewhat premature, but the facts laid out by fellow communist Vadim Zagladin have to be taken most seriously:

> The current communist movement is operating in almost 100 countries in the world. This means that the total number of communists in the world is today almost twice the number 25 years ago.[19]

The Party might be losing the competition in every area of human activities taken separately, but it is winning the overall political struggle. The communists believe that the struggle between two socioeconomic systems is primarily a political one. They believe they have the best "scientific" theory of human development, and the best political organization, for implementing this theory in practice.

Americans consider war an aberration from the normal state of affairs. Therefore, the ultimate goal in war, from the American viewpoint, is to restore the status quo and to prevent similar aberrations from happening in the future. From the Party's point of view, however, the ultimate objective of war, as an extreme form of struggle, is to secure the ultimate objective of the Party's struggle—that is, a complete monopoly on political control over the enemy's population. No residual opposition is even theoretically possible, and the re-education of the enemy's masses must be carried out without any hindrance. This presumes total control over all forms of power.

---

[18] Leonid Brezhnev, "The Great October Revolution and Human Progress," *Pravda*, November 3, 1977.

[19] CPSU Central Committee member, Vadim Zagladin, "A High International Mission: the New Addition of the CPSU Program on the World Communist Movement," *Pravda*, January 16, 1986; translated in *Foreign Broadcast Information Service* (Soviet Union), January 22, 1986, p. BB2.

In pursuing this objective, the Party seeks both to undermine the integrity of the enemy and to create an alternative power structure in the enemy's territory, while maintaining the utmost unity and mobilization on the domestic front.

In the Soviet worldview, the capitalist world constitutes a pyramid. The top of this pyramid is inhabited by the United States and its six cronies.[20] Together they exercise tight control over the rest of the developed capitalist countries, and all of them jointly control most of the Third World. China exists apart, and enjoys a special status. Between the Soviet and American pyramids, there is a small "gray area"—a "no-man's land" consisting of truly nonaligned countries. These countries are not economically, militarily, or politically integrated into the capitalist pyramid, or are trying to break away from it.

Levels of Struggle

Different methods in the Party's struggle—low-intensity, mid-intensity, and high-intensity—are applied to each part of the enemy's pyramid and to the "gray area." The high-intensity form of struggle is, of course, direct Soviet military intervention. The middle-intensity form of struggle consists of military intervention by proxies (including Party-led insurgencies) and large-scale terrorism. The low-intensity form of struggle includes a whole host of nonmilitary methods, such as economic, political, psychological, and ideological subversion, and terrorism. As a rule, the lower a country is in the enemy's pyramid, the "hotter" are the methods of struggle waged on its territory. The most violent methods are used against the members of the Soviet pyramid itself. Thus, for example, only when Afghanistan was perceived by the Party as part of its own bloc did direct military intervention become possible.

As far as the leading capitalist countries are concerned, the Party believes that they contain within themselves all the necessary seeds of their destruction. They are not the seeds of classic Marxist "class antagonism," however, but rather a dazzling array of irreconcilable contradictions and enmities between different religions, cultures, races, economic groupings, and so on. This diversity of forces and factions makes manipulation, disinformation, sabotage, recruitment, terrorism, and other forms of political struggle much more effective than military or other high-intensity methods.

[20] Take this typical assertion: "This lie [about a Soviet military menace] and these assertions [about Soviet military superiority] are used to bring political pressure to bear on the USA's Western allies, which sometimes act like a herd of sheep that has escaped from the careful control of the shepherd, who, of course, is the United States of America." (27th Congress of the CPSU on "Imperialism's Aggressive Policy," A. Sovetov, *International Affairs*, No. 8, Moscow, 1986).

The Role of Military and Technology Matters

It is difficult to underestimate the importance of technological and military matters in the overall Party's struggle. In addition to their main (specifically violent) role, they also have tremendous ideological and psychological functions. This results from the influence they have on the hearts and minds of people. Technological and military innovations can captivate the imagination of many, and induce the greatest admiration for the nations which have produced them. At the same time, they can generate the greatest fear, indignation, or hatred, which may result in either paralysis or mobilization. These psychological and ideological functions of military and technological matters have, from the Party's viewpoint, gained greatly in importance since the invention of nuclear weapons.

When one looks at the ninety-year record of the Party's struggle, one cannot help notice that the Party has killed several times as many of its own people by "peaceful means"—such as famine, collectivization, or purges—than its armed forces have killed in wars against other nations. That is, even the direct function of the military—destruction of the enemy—was largely taken over by the "quiet methods" of the Secret Police. Moreover, the Party is clearly reluctant to use direct military means against strong opponents. Nevertheless, all major gains in the Party's domain have been achieved with the help of its armed forces.

In sum, the Party considers the use of military force as a highly efficient, quick method of resolving political problems, but, on the other hand, as the most risky one.

Features of Soviet Military Doctrine

The Party has a highly elaborate military doctrine, based on the "science of war." This doctrine predicts that the socialist system will inevitably triumph in armed conflict. The Party's claim to sole possession of the "science of war" is easily proved ridiculous. Yet, it serves the sole purpose of legitimizing the Party's tight control over military affairs, because "only the combined wisdom of the Party can possess the knowledge of this 'science'." Several features of Soviet military doctrine, however, must be considered most seriously. They are instrumental in understanding Soviet military concerns about SDI.

Surprise Attack

Perhaps because the Soviet system itself is poorly equipped to deal with surprises—a fact demonstrated many times—Soviet military doctrine places a high premium on surprise attack. One of the most recent Soviet books on American strategy had this to say on the subject:

> Soviet military science proceeds from the premise that surprise, as a principle of military art, constitutes an important link in the general chain of its principles, and that their skillful application constitutes a decisive condition for the attainment of success in the armed struggle.[21]

Moreover, as a famous Soviet author claims, "The importance of the principle of surprise increases as the means of warfare develop. . . ."[22]

Soviet authors give a long list of reasons why surprise holds such importance: "Surprise permits one to catch the enemy unaware, paralyze his will, sharply reduce his combat effectiveness, disorganize his superior forces."[23] This is a clear expression of an important feature of the Soviet mentality, the mixture of paranoia and aggressiveness responsible for the worst nightmares of Soviet military planners. It is also directly connected to another principle of Soviet military doctrine, the monopoly of the initiative.

Monopoly of the Initiative

To be the first to take action, to change course, to undertake a maneuver, to introduce a new type of weapon, is one of the key principles of any struggle. It has, moreover, a paramount importance in the struggle against a vastly superior enemy. The Party is waging precisely this kind of struggle—against an overwhelmingly superior enemy, without reliable allies, in a totally hostile environment.

Sixty-five years ago, Lenin described the Party's situation this way:

> In compact group, tightly holding each other's hands, we are walking along a treacherous and difficult path. We are surrounded by enemies on all sides, and we almost always have to go under their fire.[24]

Today, in the Party's view, the situation is essentially the same. The Party's forces are always stretched too thin; communication lines are always overextended; its structure is too complex, bulky, and rigid for quick and flexible reaction; its people are always less reliable than what they seem to be when everything is normal. Hence, initiative on the part of the enemy always results in a very uncomfortable situation for the Party, given that it has to

---

[21] M. M. Kirian, *Surprise in the Military Operations of the Armed Forces of the USA* (Moscow: *Voenizdat*, 1982), p. 3.

[22] V. Ye. Savkin, *The Basic Principles of Operational Art and Tactics* (Moscow: *Voenizdat*, 1972), translated and published by the U.S. Air Force, p. 282.

[23] Savkin, ibid.

[24] V. I. Lenin, *Polnoye Sobranie Sochineniy* (*The Complete Collected Works*), (Moscow: *Politizdat*, 1965), Vol. 6, p. 249.

act from a position of inferiority. In contrast, taking the initiative permits careful planning, the concentration of forces, the mobilization of resources, choosing the right moment and place to attack, allowing time for deception operations, and the precalculation of the enemy's reaction. It also leaves room for retreat and for trying again.

Offensive Orientation

Soviet military thinking is highly offensive in nature. The Soviet people in general, and the leadership in particular, were extremely impressed by Nazi Germany's blitzkrieg during the summer of 1941. They were also much inspired by their own offensive against the Japanese at the close of World War II. All Soviet literature on military operational art is permeated with terms like "upholding the high tempo of offensive," "lightning strikes," "recapturing the initiative," " overwhelming the enemy," "deep penetration," and so on. Some Western theories about the advantages of defense over offense are scornfully rejected by the Soviets as either foolhardy or clever disinformation. However, we should not confuse the Soviet passion for offense with a disregard for defensive measures.

There are other reasons for the aggressiveness of Soviet political thinking, apart from the obvious operational advantages of imposing one's will on the enemy. Surprisingly, perhaps, it may in large part derive from a sense of mistrust toward its own population, or from the fear that being on the defensive is likely to lead to strains, cracks, and eventually the disintegration of domestic unity. The Party believes that people can most easily be controlled when they are in flux. Once movement is finished and the offensive comes to a halt, all opposition forces immediately activate and work toward the Party's defeat. Thus the strategy of the Party's struggle is conservative and risk-avoiding, yet consistently active and expansionist at the same time. The Strategic Defense Initiative of the United States has, for the first time in many years, forced the Party to react. Moreover, it must do so in its weakest areas—the economy and technology.

2.
The Military and Ideological Consequences of SDI

There have been three major stages in the Party's struggle: the local, continental, and global phases. These in turn have been related to three major events—the Bolshevik takeover in Russia, the victory over Nazi Germany, and the creation of nuclear-tipped intercontinental ballistic missiles (ICBMs). The deployment of ballistic missile defenses by the United States and its European allies could become the fourth critical event in the history of the Party's struggle. Such a development could conceivably reduce the Soviet Union to the level of a regional power once again. Moreover, if the military-technical gap continues to grow between Western countries and Japan on the one hand, and the Soviet Union on the other, then in the remote future the Soviet Union might eventually be reduced to the status of a local power. This prospect should be taken into consideration by the leaders of the Western Alliance.

In the eyes of the Soviet leadership, never before have the "imperialist forces" undertaken such a long-term and profound initiative. It is likely to have far greater ramifications than American policymakers may have originally envisioned. Directly and indirectly, the Soviet Union will be affected militarily, economically, ideologically, and socially. SDI thus amounts to an extremely serious political challenge to the Soviet leaders, one which might have implications for the Soviet political system itself.

Official Soviet Claims

In determining the actual concerns of the Soviet leadership with regard to SDI, it is worthwhile to examine briefly Soviet official claims. The Soviet leadership's reaction to the March 23, 1983 address in which President Reagan first put forward the Strategic Defense Initiative program was swift and sharp. Three days after the president's speech, Soviet leader Yuri Andropov said that American intentions were:

> . . . to acquire a first nuclear strike capability, to secure for itself the possibility of destroying—with the help of missile defenses—the corresponding strategic

systems of the other side, that is, of rendering it incapable of a retaliatory strike. This is a bid to disarm the Soviet Union in the face of the U.S. nuclear threat.[25]

Since then, two more General Secretaries of the CPSU, dozens of Soviet spokesmen, scientists, and high military figures, have made hundreds of statements concerning SDI. These statements contain nine central ideas:

1. The United States seeks military superiority, thereby jeopardizing the extant relationship of strategic nuclear parity.
2. SDI will undermine the arms control process.
3. SDI will leave computers, not human beings, in charge of mankind's fate.
4. A one-hundred percent leak-proof BMD is technically impossible.
5. The United States is trying to militarize space.
6. The United States is seeking to acquire a first-strike capability.
7. SDI will increase the probability of accidental nuclear war.
8. SDI will threaten Soviet space assets.
9. SDI will threaten, from space, Soviet installations on the ground.

As is the case with almost all Soviet public statements, these claims are not blatant lies. Each contains a grain of truth: the first seven claims a lesser degree, the last two a greater degree. However, all of them have been presented by the Soviet leadership without reference to the Party's struggle, thus making them utterly deceiving.

It is quite uncharacteristic for the Party to analyze important matters in isolation, and not in the larger context of its general political goals. Therefore, by diligently drawing the attention of Western public opinion only to the military aspects of SDI, the Soviet leadership is attempting to exploit a characteristic feature of the American mentality. Most Western critics of SDI, particularly Americans, have great difficulty grasping the interrelationships between the military, economic, psychological, and ideological aspects of international issues. Instead, Americans tend to compartmentalize a problem and analyze it piece by piece. By doing so, Western critics of SDI play into Soviet hands. The Party always looks at any problem—including SDI—first and foremost in terms of its importance in the long-term political struggle between the two sociopolitical systems. If in considering the question of the Soviet Union's response to SDI we do not consider the context of the Party's general struggle, we are bound to reach an intellectual impasse. We will not understand why the Soviets consider SDI an offensive program while we conceive of it as defensive, why they insist that it will increase the danger of nuclear conflict and be destabilizing, and why, in general, the

[25] Yurl Andropov, interview with *Pravda* Correspondent, *Pravda*, March 27, 1983.

Party does not see anything to be gained by ridding mankind of the threat of nuclear holocaust.

Soviet official claims need to be supplemented by placing them in the context of the party's view of the international environment. The Party's worldview has been well expressed in one of its latest pronouncements on the nature of international conflicts, which states:

> The new epoch which began with the October Socialist Revolution is characterized by the transition from capitalism to socialism. During this period one can distinguish four types of antagonistic relationships:
>
> 1. between socialist and capitalist sociopolitical systems (states);
>
> 2. between the working class and all working people in antagonistic societies on the one hand, and the ruling classes of those societies on the other hand;
>
> 3. between peoples fighting for their national liberation, as well as those who have embarked on the path of independent development, and imperialist states, which pursue colonial and neocolonial policy; and
>
> 4. between capitalist states.[26]

This book was written for the officer corps by sixteen of the highest military authorities on Soviet military doctrine and strategy, most of them generals. It cannot be dismissed as sheer rhetoric. How then should one interpret its strange assertions? Why does it ignore obvious sources of conflict such as those based on purely economic, religious, national, or racial antagonisms? Why does it exclude from consideration conflicts between socialist countries?

It may simply be embarrassing to admit that socialist China can fight socialist Vietnam without any interference from imperialist forces; perhaps it is possible to dismiss the war between Iran and Iraq, now raging in its seventh year, as insignificant. But why are the conflicts and antagonisms presented in such a way that they are all directed against the capitalist system? This is the most interesting question posed by the book cited above.

Note that according to this point of view, everyone—the socialist countries, working people, "people fighting for national liberation"—are all fighting against capitalism. Moreover, the capitalist countries are fighting among themselves. In other words, Soviet strategists exclude (or simply ignore as minor or insignificant) many sources of international conflict; the remaining political forces are arranged so that all are arrayed against the "capitalists." In this interpretation, the Party is positioned at the head of an overwhelmingly superior alliance of political forces; the capitalists have no chance. This Soviet assessment of the nature of international conflict and the correlation

[26] D. A. Volkogonov, ed. *Marksistsko-Leninskoye Uchenie o Voine i Armii* (*Marxist-Leninist Teaching About War and the Armed Forces*) (Moscow: Voenizdat, 1984), p. 41-42.

of political forces needs to be kept in mind when examining official Soviet objections to SDI.

Superiority

If a neutral observer accepts the Party's point of view, he might legitimately ask: Why should not the greatly outnumbered capitalists seek actively to defend themselves through the best means available to them—military-technical superiority? If, as the Party holds, the whole world is fighting the capitalists (that is, the "whole world" of socialist countries, people "fighting for liberation" in the Third World, and working people in the capitalist countries), why indeed should the Soviet leadership complain that the imperialist countries are striving for military-technical superiority? Thus, in a typical statement, Soviet Defense Minister Sergei Sokolov has charged: "The Pentagon is now rushing into space. What for? Once again to attempt to achieve military superiority over the USSR, this time through space."[27]

The answer is that the Soviet leaders consider the quest for military superiority to be their indisputable prerogative, as explained in the *Soviet Military Encyclopedia*:

> Strengthening the defense capabilities of the USSR and all countries of the socialist camp requires ensuring military-technical superiority over the armed forces of the imperialists, the aggressive blocs . . . Soviet military doctrine determines the direction of preparing the country and the armed forces for repulsing aggression, provides a program of action for ensuring military-technical superiority over the armed forces of the probable enemies.[28]

Anyone familiar with Soviet military literature knows that, in the eyes of the Party, striving for military-technical superiority is a sacred duty—the most natural and important part of the competition between two systems. However, as the Party is aware, striving for superiority is considered useless by some Westerners. Therefore, by condemning the Western attempt to acquire superiority, the Party is trying to win supporters for its political campaign against SDI.

Parity

The theme of military parity is a totally new one for Soviet propaganda. In the late 1970s, Soviet mass publications stopped mentioning superiority

---

[27] Answers of the USSR Defense Minister, Marshal S. L. Sokolov, to *Tass* correspondent, *Krasnaya Zvezda*, May 5, 1985.

[28] *Sovetskaya Voennaya Entsyclopedia* (Moscow: Voenizdat, 1976), Vol. 2, p. 253.

as a goal and switched to emphasizing strategic parity. Thus, as the late Yuri Andropov said:

The attainment of military-strategic parity between socialism and capitalism was one of the most important results of the last several decades. It took great resources and effort on the part of our people and the peoples of other countries of the socialist commonwealth to achieve this parity.[29]

This tactical switch occurred, not accidentally, in the middle of the SALT II negotiations; it should have been too transparent to deceive anybody. However, there is an even more important reason why the Party seems to have become content with the concept of military parity between the two superpowers.

From the Party's point of view, the correlation of forces shifted in favor of the socialist system in the mid-1970s. As discussed in the preceding chapter, the Soviet political mentality considers every form of power to be convertible into political power; therefore, when the Party speaks of the correlation of forces, it means ultimately the correlation of political forces. Military force, although extremely important, is still only one among the many forces determining the overall correlation. In the Party's reasoning, military-strategic parity negates the overall economic, human, technological, and geographical advantages of the West while liberating the huge political forces of the Soviet bloc. In other words, nuclear-strategic parity frees the Party to pursue its struggle by all other means in a calm, calculated and persistent manner. It gives the Party time to plan, develop and allocate its resources, choose its priorities, try different approaches, correct mistakes, and try again.

The Arms Control Process

The concept of controlling the arms race by diplomatic means also needs to be examined from the Party's standpoint. In its view, the military buildup of the Soviet Union and its allies—which has always been under the strictest possible control of the Party—cannot be placed under even the marginal control of anybody else, especially that of the "imperialists." Instead, it is the "military-industrial complexes of the imperialists" that long ago got out of hand; they must now be controlled by "peace-loving people" in order to destroy imperialism and thereby banish wars once and for all. Soviet doctrine states:

Imperialism is the fundamental source of all wars of our time. Only with the victory of socialism and the departure from the historic arena of imperialism,

[29] *Materialy Plenuma Tsentralnogo Comiteta KPSS* (Materials of the Plenum of the Central Committee of the CPSU), Moscow, June 14-15, 1983, p. 25.

the last system of exploitation, will the basis, the main source of wars, be eliminated on the planet.[30]

The essence of the arms control process lies, therefore, in controlling or restraining the "imperialist forces," rendering them unable to resist efforts to eliminate them. "Peace-loving people" should help the imperialists "depart from the historic arena," after which peace will reign in the world. Apparently, the arms control process has obviously been going well during the last twenty-five years from the Party's point of view, if only because the prospect of its disruption has caused the Party great concern. Indeed, during the years of arms control, the Soviet Union has moved from a position of overwhelming strategic nuclear inferiority in the early 1960s into a position of parity in the mid-1970s, and was heading toward a position of superiority at the beginning of the 1980s. Therefore, the Party would be only too happy to have another quarter of a century of similar "arms control" progress.

Computers in Charge

The Party argument against computers—essentially the allegation that these devices threaten to remove human control over vital defense decisionmaking processes—reflects the complex attitude of the Soviet political mentality toward technological progress in general, and computers in particular. The Soviet mentality worships technological progress, and the Party would of course be glad to see the Soviet Union first and best in every area of scientific-technological development—as long as these technological innovations enhanced and secured the Party's leading role.

Until fairly recently, the Party demonstrated great skill in utilizing technical innovations to increase its control over the masses. Since Stalin's death, the Party has been captivated by the idea of a network of supercomputers helping to control production, distribution, and information flow. As with other technological innovations—such as radio, television, newspapers, the cinema, printing technology and copying machines—the Party planned to use computers first and foremost for the purpose of controlling and reeducating the citizenry in line with its ideal. (Every typewriter in the country, for example, has been registered and its "signature" recorded with the KGB, which helps it analyze underground pamphlets in an effort to determine their authors.) And, from the Party's point of view, computers have so far been very helpful in fulfilling these tasks. Today, however, circumstances require the Party, in the interest of technological progress (and, ultimately, in the interest of retaining its control), to allow computers to the masses—and, in consequence, the tools to spread information. The Party thus faces

[30] *Marxist-Leninist Teaching on War and the Armed Forces*, p. 20.

a painful dilemma: how to utilize so powerful a tool as computer technology for the purpose of reeducation, while ensuring against its use for "counterrevolutionary" purposes.

There is another ideological paradox connected to computers. The Party claims to comprise the best minds and truest hearts of the nation, ready to sacrifice for the good of humanity. Naturally, only they can be entrusted with such deadly weapons as nuclear missiles—surely not lesser mortals, as yet not possessed of a proletarian class consciousness. But on this argument, computers are even less suited to be charged with resolving the socialist-capitalist feud—for they have no conscience at all. Moreover, if computers are in charge, the Party will not be sure about the outcome of the struggle. The two political systems involved are far more sophisticated than any computers. Indeed, because it cannot produce the best computers—and because capitalist computers are not programmed with a proletariat-class consciousness—the uncertainty inherent in giving the power of decision to a machine presents an unacceptable risk.

In sum, when Western opponents of SDI and the Soviet leadership oppose the increasing role of computers in military affairs, they are concerned about entirely different—indeed, in many ways *opposite*—matters. Western critics are concerned with dehumanizing and over-centralizing the process of vital decisionmaking. The Party, in contrast, is concerned with the erosion of its monopoly on information and, therefore, of its power.

Technical Feasibility

Arguments about the impossibility of achieving a "one hundred percent leak-proof" BMD system are largely demagogic; few things in the world are one hundred percent effective. The best, most expensive car in the world is still less than perfect, and yet it would be ridiculous to demand that its manufacturer make it perfect. Assessing the feasibility of an efficient BMD system from the Soviet point of view is a very important element in analyzing possible Soviet reactions to SDI. In this regard, it is worth noting that if any group in the world believes American scientists and engineers can build a close-to-one hundred percent leakproof BMD system, it is Soviet scientists. The Party shares this respect for American technical prowess and industrial potential. Therefore, when scientists and advisers to the Central Committee of the CPSU say that Americans can build an SDI system, the Party has every reason to believe them. Judging from the Party's reaction to the President's March 23, 1983 address, it does indeed.

The Militarization of Space

Space was militarized by the Soviet Union thirty years ago, long before the first nonmilitary missions were flown. The Soviet Union still does not have an equivalent to NASA, the U.S. civilian space agency; Soviet space programs have been run entirely by the military. As early as eighteen years ago, Marshal V. D. Sokolovsky provided the rationale for the need to militarize space:

> Soviet military strategy takes into account the need for studying the question of the use of outer space and aerospace vehicles. This must be done to ensure the safety of our country, in the interest of all socialist cooperation, for the preservation of peace in the world.[31]

According to the U.S. Department of Defense, the Soviet Union has launched an average of about one hundred rockets annually during the last six years. Eighty to ninety percent of these have had at least partially military purposes. Of course, this is as much an indication of Soviet technological inferiority as it is of devotion to capturing the ultimate "high ground." Soviet intelligence satellites last only several weeks—rather than months, as do American satellites—because methods of collecting and recovering intelligence data are amazingly expensive and outdated. Launching one hundred satellites a year probably costs the Soviet Union, by rough estimation, fifteen billion dollars annually.

Judging from the attention and resources the Party invests in space activities, it is obviously convinced that space will indeed be the ultimate high ground, where the last and decisive battle between socialism and capitalism is most likely to take place.

A First Nuclear Strike

The Soviet leadership claims that the United States is trying to achieve a first-strike nuclear capability by pursuing SDI. It is doubtful that this claim represents genuine Soviet concerns. At least twice during the last thirty-five years the United States has held overwhelming nuclear superiority, and the consequent ability to inflict a devastating strategic defeat on the Soviet Union. Moreover, the United States first had this advantage at the height of Soviet-U.S. hostility during the Cold War, when the Soviet Union had just acquired nuclear weapons but did not have the means to deliver them. The United States did not press its advantage nearly to the extent that it might have. The very low level of readiness of Soviet nuclear forces—much lower than

[31] V. D. Sokolovsky, *Military Strategy*, 3rd edition (Moscow, 1968). Translated by Harriet Fast Scott as *Soviet Military Strategy* (New York: Crane Russak and Company, Inc., 1975), p. 458.

those of the United States—testifies to the lack of Soviet concern about a preemptive American nuclear strike "out of the blue." This relative discrepancy continues, despite the fact that the pyramidal Soviet control structure is very vulnerable to even a limited nuclear strike.[32]

The Soviet leadership knows that so long as only a few Soviet nuclear weapons are capable of reaching American soil, no American administration would take the risk of launching a nuclear attack—regardless of how devastating it might be for the Soviet Union.

Instability

Both Western and Soviet critics of SDI claim that deployment of an American BMD system will increase strategic instability. However, these two groups express quite different ideas with the same terms. The Soviets claim that militarizing space and delegating more decisionmaking responsibility to computers will increase the chances of accidental nuclear war. Westerners, when they speak of strategic instability, mean mostly that the Soviet leaders—fearing the possibility of SDI effectively disarming them—might resort to a preemptive nuclear strike.

Both arguments are superficial, to say the least. However, while the Soviet propagandists' intentions are fairly clear, the Western critics obviously have not thought the matter through. First of all, an SDI system would be designed for the purpose of shooting down enemy rockets, not for launching rockets. If no rockets are launched, therefore, nothing will happen. Secondly, even a limited ballistic missile defense would be an indispensable mechanism for dealing at least with one nuclear escalation scenario. As was demonstrated during the KAL 007 shootdown, the Soviet military machine has become far too complicated to handle fast-developing crisis situations by funneling information through political channels. In other words, the gap between the commanders of military districts and the Politburo is growing larger; it is therefore conceivable that, in some future situations, the Soviet military may take actions not in accord with the Politburo's will.

This means that an American SDI system might well serve the purpose of saving the Soviet leadership from itself—or, more accurately, from the actions of its own military. In any one of a number of unlikely, yet grave, scenarios—a crazy Soviet general, or another (more serious) submarine accident, to cite only two—an effective SDI could relieve Soviet leaders of the obligation to decide whether to fight a nuclear war. It seems certain that

[32] See Harriet and William Scott, *The Soviet Control Structure: Capabilities for Wartime Survival* (New York: Crane Russak, 1983), pp. 135-138; also John M. Weinstein, "All Features Grate and Stall: Soviet Strategic Vulnerabilities and the Future of Deterrence," in *Defense of the West*, Robert Kennedy and John M. Weinstein, eds. (Boulder, Colorado: Westview Press, 1984), pp. 56, 62.

the Kremlin's occupants are not unaware of the alternative SDI might provide to what now could only become a very painful situation indeed.

Finally, with the introduction of a global command-control-communication and intelligence (C^3I) system, based on many highly sensitive and mutually complementary sensors, the identification of every flying object would be close to absolute. This diminishes the chance of mistakes so characteristic of the past. Even if an SDI system were to make a mistake and shoot down a nonmilitary rocket of the enemy, there would be no need for either side to alert their strategic forces or consider a possible retaliatory nuclear strike. As far as a Soviet preemptive nuclear strike is concerned, the deployment of an American SDI system could only make this less probable. This is especially true if deployment starts with a C^3I system, begins as soon as possible, and proceeds gradually over a long period of time.

The Soviets now need up to a week to disable or completely destroy all U.S. and NATO low-earth orbit intelligence satellites, a prerequisite of any full-scale nuclear attack on the United States.[33] An initial deployment of enhanced C^3I capabilities, as the first effort in a BMD, would increase the time required for a Soviet first strike to perhaps several weeks. This would necessitate dozens of launches of Soviet satellite killers daily for several days, perhaps weeks. The U.S. BMD system would have enough time to place its defense and retaliatory forces on alert, to knock down several of the most important Soviet communication and intelligence satellites, to replace some of its own satellites, and to take other measures. In other words, if the military operations of both sides grow more dependent on complicated space systems, then the initial hostilities required to set the stage for full-scale war would have to start in space. If things should ever come to this, it would certainly be better to skirmish in space rather than on the ground or at sea. Enough time might be had to settle the dispute before it got out of hand.

Finally, the development of an extremely sophisticated C^3I system connected with SDI would not only reduce the chances of a Soviet surprise nuclear attack on the United States; it would similarly make an invasion of Western Europe—or anywhere else, for that matter—less likely. Without the advantage of surprise attack, the conquest of Western Europe would be much too difficult, if not impossible. In the words of Christopher N. Donnelly, a well-known British authority on Soviet military affairs:

> . . . if the required favourable political circumstances do not exist, and if the Soviet Union is not convinced of its ability to achieve surprise or a rapid end to the war, then the Russians will never start a war in Europe.[34]

---

[33] See Thomas H. Krebs, "The Soviet Space Threat," *National Center for Policy Analysis* (Dallas, June 1984).

[34] *International Defense Review*, No. 12/1981.

We cannot agree more, except that we would refer to our adversaries as Soviets, not Russians.

In sum, the first seven official Soviet claims concerning SDI do not represent true Soviet concerns and fears. The last two, concerning the threat to Soviet space and ground assets as well as some implicit ideological concerns of the party, deserve closer attention. They reflect the real military fears of the Soviet leadership more than the rest.

The Party's Ideological and Psychological Concerns

The Role of Fear

Not surprisingly, perhaps the Party does not talk about its fear that it might lose its status as a global power. It sees, however, that if the fear of nuclear annihilation one day dissipates, exactly this might result. It took the Party twenty-four years, from 1897 to 1921, to seize power in Russia and thus to become a local power. It took the same amount of time, from 1921 to 1945, for it to become a regional power. It took only another ten years, however, for the Soviet Union to become a global power, both politically and militarily. One might say this last development was somewhat premature. The Soviet economy had just finished its recovery from the devastation of the Second World War; the Party was still in the midst of consolidating its grip over Eastern Europe. The revolts in East Germany in 1953, and in Poland and Hungary in 1956, testify that the consolidation of Soviet power in those countries was not yet complete when the Soviet Union successfully tested its first intercontinental ballistic missile—and thereby acquired the capability to threaten the "citadel of imperialism."

Being a global power means that a country has the ability to project its influence to any part of the globe, though the means of doing so can vary tremendously. Great Britain, for example, projected her power through the attractiveness of her parliamentary and judicial systems, and by her industrial strength and (chiefly naval) military presence. The United States projects its influence around the world through the attractiveness of its democracy, its economic and technological achievements, its culture and lifestyle, and by its military presence—primarily its air force, navy, and nuclear missile forces. However, the Soviet presence in the world is manifested through completely different means. The Soviet Union is very unusual in being—as many have described it—a one-dimensional global power. One might say that the Soviet Union exports only two items: Marxist ideals and the fear of nuclear annihilation. In addition, the Party clandestinely "smuggles" out all sorts of dissatisfactions, disturbances, and revolutionary movements—known among Soviet strategists as part of the process of "softening up the enemy."

In the Soviet political mentality, evil desires and fears are much more powerful forces than, say, love and altruism. The Party believes that by inducing the right amount of fear in the masses it can always achieve a desirable result. Fear of the enemy can mobilize and unite the population, and increase their sacrifices; fear of reprisals can increase the productivity of the Soviet economy, paralyze domestic opposition, and so on. Fear is the glue that holds society together, and the engine that drives it forward. Fear, from the Party's point of view, is equally effective in exporting revolution. Fear of Big Brother's intervention installed the communist parties of Eastern Europe, and has kept them in power. Fear of nuclear annihilation can paralyze the enemy, creating a mood of "better Red than dead." The new General Secretary, Mikhail Gorbachev, seems convinced of the effectiveness of this tool. He never misses an opportunity to remind Westerners that:

> . . . today, more than ever before, it is necessary to be vigilant with regard to the machinations of those who are pushing the world toward an abyss, this time a nuclear one.[35]

The antinuclear movement, from Britain to New Zealand to Massachusetts, testifies to the effectiveness of these efforts. Perhaps one of the most amusing things for the Soviets to watch has been the utterly ridiculous debate in the West about a so-called "nuclear winter." The expenditure of so much energy and passion on this question on both sides of the political spectrum has served Soviet interests well. Yet the nuclear winter debate, at least in the United States, managed once again to exacerbate partisan biases to the level of hatred, divide the country, and increase pressures on the government—whose efforts are directed exactly against the occurrence of any kind of nuclear death, whether from radiation or from a nuclear winter.

Considering the effectiveness of fear as an instrument in softening up the enemy, the Party is naturally concerned about the prospect of being deprived of this tool. Even low-intensity methods of softening the enemy might become less efficient if the Party lost its ability to support the right level of nuclear fear.[36]

The Role of Rockets and Space

Sometimes Westerners who are skeptical about the global ambitions of the Soviet Communist Party raise a legitimate question: Why does the conventional power of the Soviet Union remain largely limited to the Eur-

[35] *New York Times*, May 10, 1985.

[36] An excellent and still very relevant study on the Party's strategy and technique of low-intensity conflict is the classic study by Robert Strausz-Hupe, William R. Kintner, James E. Dougherty, and Alvin J. Cottrell, *Protracted Conflict.* (New York: Harper Colophon Books, 1958.)

asian continent? If it seeks world domination, how can it expect to achieve this without amphibious ships, aircraft carriers, strategic airlift, and the other capabilities necessary to invade and occupy countries? Is this not proof of the Party's defensive intentions? The answer lies in the limited industrial resources of the Party on the one hand, and the unconventional methods of the Party's struggle on the other.

As early as 1937, Stalin issued an order to build an aircraft carrier.[37] It is worth noting that this decision to build a politically prestigious and very expensive military item was made just a few years after the most devastating famine in Russian history, during which at least six million peasants died of starvation. The country's resources have always been strained to the utmost degree, and the first full-fledged Soviet carrier is still under construction. But, despite shortcomings and constraints, the Party has steadily and persistently increased its military presence around the world. It has built heavy lift aircraft, like the Condor; built up its marine corps; it is building aircraft carriers, a navy of enormous size, and is encouraging new weapons research. Unless the Party actually means what it says in claiming world domination as its goal, it is unclear exactly why the defense of the Soviet Union requires these capabilities.

Space presented the Party with the unique opportunity to project its power all over the world in a relatively inexpensive manner. One aircraft carrier costs several billion dollars, yet can show the flag in only one port at a time. One Sputnik, or a man in space, inculcates strong respect and fear of the Soviet Union everywhere—while costing perhaps ten times less. Space has become, in a sense, the path by which the Soviet Union has taken a shortcut to global power status. In the eyes of the Soviet people, the conquest of space is a symbol of victory over territory and boundaries that were not fully conquered even by aviation. After all, the Soviet people cannot travel abroad; many parts of their country still remain inaccessible. It is only a slight exaggeration to say that the Soviet Union leapt into the cosmos before building roads. This was an example of superior Soviet strategic thinking at work. Now, however—to pursue this metaphor—the Party must build roads if it wants to compete successfully in space. This is a frustrating prospect for the Soviet leadership, considering the almost total absence of roads in the Soviet Union. Only the West can help the Soviets maintain the illusion of Soviet equality or even supremacy in space.

When a series of Western space disasters occurred in early 1986, the Party decided to exploit what it saw as an opportunity to reestablish Soviet supremacy in space—at least in the eyes of world public opinion. This had been lost during the 1960s. Perhaps for this reason alone, Soviet authorities

[37] Nikolai Kuznetsov, *Nakanune* (Moscow: Voenizdat, 1966), p. 258, quoted in Robert Bathurst's *Understanding the Soviet Navy: A Handbook* (Newport, R.I.: Naval War College Press, 1979), p. 10.

televised the Soviet space station launch in June 1986. Predictably, some Western observers reacted in awe: "The Soviets are so far ahead of the United States in space experience that they are almost out of sight," wrote Gerinald Turnhill. "Clearly, the Soviets are ahead of us in space operational areas," said Marcia S. Smith, president of the American Astronautical Society.[38] Of course, "far ahead in space experience" and "ahead in space operational areas" are relatively narrow technical judgments. They are a far cry from the results of polls taken among West Europeans shortly after the launch of the first two Sputniks, when five times as many Frenchmen, three times as many Britons, and twice as many Italians thought that the Soviet Union was "ahead of the United States in scientific development" than those who thought the reverse.[39] Since then, of course, Americans have achieved a number of most remarkable firsts in space exploration. In addition, the British and French beat the Soviets in the Concorde/TU-44 race; they might surpass the Soviets in competition for building a space shuttle as well. The Japanese, meanwhile, are indisputably ahead of the Soviets in high technology, and could become a first-rank aerospace nation in the 1990s, when they plan to launch a manned space station, land an unmanned spacecraft on the moon, and build their own shuttle.[40] Even the Chinese have announced their intention to launch a manned spacecraft. Their close technological cooperation with the United States may give the Soviet leadership a bigger headache than SDI itself.

The Party desperately needs another space spectacular to impress world opinion and overcome the talk about a fifteen-year lag behind the United States in computers and the like.[41] It needs something like an expedition to Mars—and, indeed, there are already reports that preparation for such an effort are underway. It would be a serious American strategic mistake to let the Soviets take a lead in the exploration of space, even for a short period of time.

Soviet Military Fears

Though the imperialists' resources vastly exceed their own, the Party holds that two factors have kept them from crushing the socialist system: nuclear weapons, and the invulnerable political structure of the socialist camp. Both these factors may be affected by SDI. Even before President Reagan's March 1983 address on SDI, the Soviet leadership began to sound

[38] *Washington Post*, June 30, 1986.

[39] Joseph M. Goldsen, ed. *Outer Space in World Politics* (New York: Praeger, 1963), p. 76.

[40] *Aviation Week and Space Technology*, July 14, 1986.

[41] See, for example, an excellent article "Communism vs. the Computer" by Rex Malik, *Computerworld*, July 9, 1984.

somewhat apocalyptic. Perhaps the most striking example was Marshal Ogarkov's pamphlet, "Always Ready to Defend the Fatherland," published in 1982. It called for "total military preparedness not only by the armed forces and military industries, but also of all sectors of the economy, the Party, and civil defense."[42] It is difficult, if not impossible, to explain these fears as the result of an increase in concern about the probability of nuclear war. There is little reason to think that this probability had increased significantly during the preceding five to seven years. The reasons must be sought elsewhere.

The Question of Leadership's Vulnerability

In the Party's view, every war in human history has followed the same pattern: one crushes the military backbone and industrial muscle of the adversary, breaks its morale, and overcomes the resistance of its population, until finally one can strike at the brain of the enemy—that is, its political leadership. Only after the enemy's leadership has been supplanted by a more compliant one can the goals of the war be attained. The leadership of a nation has always been the best protected part of the enemy's forces, and therefore the most difficult one to strike. One can understand, then, why the Soviet leadership is unquestionably the best protected government in the world, thoroughly insulated from both external and internal threats.

The first challenge to this view of the progress of war appeared with the invention of aircraft and tanks. Some strategists thought that surgical strikes from the air or by tank columns would make war impossible because the leaders of belligerent nations—not populations, industry, or even armies—would be the prime targets of strategic strikes. However, both tanks and airplanes were slow and noisy enough to provide sufficient warning time for the leadership. Bombing also proved quite inaccurate, and explosives were not powerful enough to destroy underground targets. Therefore, effective defenses against tanks and bombers evolved almost simultaneously with the creation of these weapons. Then, as powerful nuclear explosives were developed, the idea of striking at the enemy's brain was revived. This time, however, there was a grotesque twist: one can destroy the leadership of the enemy, but in order to achieve this one has to be ready to risk unpredictable damage—not only to one's own country but to all of mankind as well.

---

[42] *Washington Post,* March 11, 1982.

Nuclear Weapons

At the beginning, the Party was exuberant about nuclear missiles. They believed that strategic nuclear weapons satisfied two key principles of Soviet military doctrine: surprise and the offensive character of warfare. As late as 1972, an authoritative Soviet publication stated:

> A most important new qualitative feature of modern war is the possibility of directly achieving strategic results by using strategic nuclear forces, bypassing the consecutive stages of developing tactical successes into operational-level ones, and theater into strategic ones, as was the case in previous wars.[43]

Later, the Party had to admit that the military utility of nuclear weapons was limited. But it did not go so far as to embrace the point of view expressed by Hans Morgenthau:

> The destructiveness of nuclear weapons is so enormous that it overwhelms all possible objectives of rational foreign policy. If they were used as instruments of national policy, nuclear weapons would destroy the tangible objective of the policy and the belligerents as well.[44]

Contrary to Morgenthau's beliefs that nuclear weapons were largely useless, the Party found a very good use for them. While Americans attempted to use them as an instrument to restrain Soviet aggression, the Soviets used them as tools of intimidation and blackmail.

Fears of Conventional War

According to the Party's logic, immunity from nuclear attack, dominance in space, and development of new sophisticated conventional weapons might encourage the West to risk a prolonged conventional war with the purpose of eliminating the socialist political system:

> The U.S. leadership claims that by the end of the 1980s, as NATO troops are equipped with high-accuracy weapons, especially long-range intelligence-gathering and strike complexes, the real prerequisites for the bloc to wage a long conventional war in Europe will be created. Then, under the cover of its "Euro-strategic" nuclear forces (the "small nuclear umbrella"), and U.S. strategic nuclear forces (the "large nuclear umbrella"), the NATO Alliance, using only conventional strike means, will allegedly be able to achieve independently the military-political goals it has set itself in Europe. That means eliminating the socialist system in the Warsaw Pact's East European countries, considerably weakening the Soviet

---

[43] N. A. Lomov, ed. *Scientific-Technical Progress and the Revolution in Military Affairs* (Moscow: Voenizdat, 1973). Translated and published by the U.S. Air Force, p. 274.

[44] Hans J. Morgenthau, *A New Foreign Policy for the United States* (New York: Frederick Praeger, 1969), p. 208.

Union, and forcing it to give up the armed struggle on advantageous terms for the West.[45]

This is perhaps one of the most revealing official Soviet statements. A protracted conventional war against a superior enemy, with the additional danger of a potential strike to the rear, is the ultimate Soviet nightmare. These fears may appear exaggerated to Western analysts, who are aware of the tremendous conventional and nuclear might that the Soviet Union could bring to bear in the European theater—and who are also aware that NATO has no plans whatsoever to invade the Soviet bloc. But one must keep in mind the simple psychological fact that aggressive individuals (or national elites) habitually ascribe the same aggressiveness to others.

The Nonnuclear Strategic Threat

Finally, another Soviet fear is related to the current development of nonnuclear strategic weapons, which might become a very important factor at approximately the same time that an efficient BMD system might be deployed. During the last three decades, the strategic nuclear arms race has overshadowed developments in these areas, which has been proceeding without much publicity on both sides of the Iron Curtain. Many experts realized long ago that the immense destructive power of nuclear weapons made them practical only as a political tool. Although the Soviets were more optimistic than Americans about the possibility of fighting and winning a nuclear war, during the first half of the 1960s they came to the conclusion that nuclear war is not feasible as a method of resolving the mortal struggle between two sociopolitical systems:

> There is too great a risk of the destruction of one's own government, and the responsibility to humanity for the fatal consequences of nuclear war is too heavy, for an aggressor to make an easy decision on the immediate employment of nuclear weapons from the very beginning of a war without having used all other means for the attainment of its objective.[46]

From a purely military point of view, nuclear weapons are essentially useless in most scenarios. In the meantime, however, new highly powerful conventional explosives combined with precision-guided delivery systems have made it possible to achieve militarily advantageous results through the precise placement of nonnuclear charges. Richard Burt, now Ambassador of the United States to the Federal Republic of Germany, wrote in 1977:

---

[45] V. Alekseyev, *Krasnaya Zvezda*, quoted in *Foreign Broadcast Information Service* (Soviet Union), III, January 23, 1986, p. CC5.

[46] S. P. Ivanov, "Soviet Military Doctrine and Strategy," in *Voennaya Mysl'* (*Military Thought*) No. 5, May 1969; translated in *Foreign Press Digest* 0117/69, December 18, 1969, p. 48.

> . . . during the next decade, the proliferation of a new generation of precision strike systems—air- and surface-launched cruise missiles and remotely piloted vehicles—could usher in a new era of strategic conventional warfare. Armed with fuel-air explosives or advanced point munitions, these weapons would enable states to threaten intolerable damage against soft and even hard targets of an adversary without resort to nuclear blackmail . . . . While most of these missiles are not being produced for strategic missions, the guidance systems, the motors, and the airframes of many of them could be exploited for such roles.[47]

Although Burt's time assessment was perhaps too optimistic, technological developments have exceeded expectations in generating an even greater number of potential weapons for this role. In addition, the fact that there has not as yet been any U.S. defense against nuclear missiles has slowed the development of nonnuclear strategic forces. But this situation is now changing radically.

At about the time that nuclear weapons might be rendered "obsolete" by the development of SDI, new nonnuclear strategic weapons will become available. To understand the Party's fears in this regard, we have to take a closer look at the technological possibilities inherent in SDI from the viewpoint of the Party's political mentality. From this perspective, a number of technological developments are (theoretically) creating a historically unique situation, in which the leadership of a country could be endangered or even paralyzed without threatening the destruction of the main military and industrial power of the country. The technologies at issue include:

- "smart" or "brilliant" precision-guided munitions;
- space-based global information and position sytems;
- long-range delivery vehicles, including an aerospace plane;
- X-ray laser and elementary particle beam weapons placed in space;
- electronic warfare capabilities;
- superfast railguns.

The Soviet leadership is therefore likely to be uncomfortable about the nature of the threat posed by this new type of conventional warfare—much more so than it has been by the threat posed by more powerful but unwieldy nuclear weapons.

With the appearance of these new technological opportunities, the sixty-year old concept of surgical strikes is making a comeback. New, very powerful explosives, combined with new methods of delivery and guidance, are making precise strikes at the nerve centers of a country at least theoretically possible. Israel's 1985 raid on PLO headquarters in Tunis, and the American raid on Libya in April 1986, are harbingers of these new possibilities. If

[47] Richard Burt, *Nuclear Proliferation and Conventional Arms Transfers: The Missing Link*, the California Seminar on Arms Control and Foreign Policy, Discussion Paper No. 76, September 1977, p. 17.

these strikes were impressive—executed, as they were, with ten-to-fifteen-year-old technology—one can only imagine what might be possible by the turn of the century. Suddenly, the great advantage of the totally centralized Soviet system might become a tremendous strategic liability. The Soviet Union could conceivably be completely paralyzed for several weeks, perhaps months, if its control centers were simultaneously destroyed. Conversely, the more autonomous, loosely structured societies of the West, with millions of small and independent enterprises and prolific transportation networks, might prove more impervious to surgical strikes. In fact, Western societies could conceivably exist without central government for quite a long time, as Italy has demonstrated many times. Moreover, American military commanders have the capacity and authority to continue fighting on their own.

In calculating Soviet vulnerabilities, one has to take into account certain structures peculiar to the Soviet Union. The system of control (the headquarters of the party, KGB, MVD, Komsomol, Unions, and the Army) in the fifty largest industrial and administrative centers probably amounts to roughly five hundred targets. The main Soviet military storage depots add another two hundred targets.[48] The railroad system, which carries seventy-five percent of both freight and passengers, and whose total length is only half that of the American railroad system, has perhaps only fifty choke points; it could be completely paralyzed with only two hundred precisely placed high-explosive charges. The Soviet energy supply network is also integrated in one centrally run system, and could be rendered inoperable with only one hundred charges—particularly if one decided to destroy a dozen of the largest hydroelectric stations. This would stop all industry and virtually all passenger traffic in all the big cities of the country. City transport is roughly ninety percent electrically-powered, and few Soviet people have cars—to say nothing about trucks. If we add radio and television stations, and 1500 bunkers (for the elite), the total number of targets emerges as approximately three thousand.

If for every target one has to fire five charges in order to approach one hundred percent kill probability, then an attacker would need only fifteen to twenty thousand nonnuclear warheads.[49] Is this technically possible? It is certainly far more possible today than four years ago, when the following was written:

> The following technologies are eroding the monopoly of nuclear weapons: Tactical weaponry now incorporates techniques for both controlled dispersal and precise delivery of some extremely efficient munitions for penetration, fragmentation, and concussion. Space systems are providing the global information

[48] *Soviet Military Power*, 1985, pp. 70-71.

[49] For a somewhat different assessment, see the article by Thomas Powers, "Choosing a Strategy for World War Three," *The Atlantic Monthly*, Nov. 1982, p. 109. It identifies 3,543 targets; we believe industrial complexes should not be included.

necessary for precision navigation and high-capacity communication, reconnaissance, and surveillance. Strategic delivery vehicles, both aircraft and missiles, have proven their ability to transport substantial payloads rapidly and reliably over intercontinental distances. These technologies are not new, and the capabilities afforded by them are no longer highly speculative. They are all mature enough to have spawned second- and third-generation systems.[50]

The author goes on to say:

> Today there are precision-guided means of delivery which can hit the target with an accuracy of several yards, and thousands of ballistic and cruise missiles already exist.[51]

Of course, a C^3I system with global capacity, that could simultaneously identify and target separate buildings and other small objects, has yet to be developed. Even more important, surgical nonnuclear strikes will remain a purely theoretical concept as long as a retaliatory nuclear strike is possible.

It is logical to object that no American administration would ever dare to contemplate such a strategic strike. But this is beside the point: we are discussing the Soviet leadership's fears, not the actual plans of American military strategists or even the desirability of such plans. Without taking these Soviet fears and concerns into consideration, it is difficult to understand Soviet pronouncements like those contained in Marshal Ogarkov's pamphlet. More recently, *Krasnaya Zvezda* expressed similar fears, stating:

> [The NATO's plan's] thrust consists of creating military superiority over the Warsaw Pact states in conventional armaments and favorable conditions for conducting combat operations with a view of defeating opposing armed forces in the initial period of a war without using nuclear weapons.[52]

The political ramifications of a nonnuclear strategic strike would be very different from those of a nuclear attack. While a strategic nuclear strike can only scale down or ruin the Soviet pyramid, a precise nonnuclear strategic strike might substantially reshape it, by effectively decapitating it. All kinds of centrigufal forces (national, religious, and dissident) would be unleashed if the strings of power were broken or severed; undoubtedly, the numerical superiority of the masses over the elite would come into play. This could be deliberately exacerbated by careful targeting. X-ray lasers and superfast rail guns placed in space could lead to even more discriminating weapons in the distant future. These might virtually force the leadership into hiding, thus promoting an even greater gap between the rulers and the ruled than now exists.

---

[50] Carl H. Builder, "Strategic Conflict Without Nuclear Weapons," Rand Corporation Report #R-2980—FF/RC, 1983, p. 13.

[51] Ibid., p. 24.

[52] *Foreign Broadcast Information Service* (Soviet Union), December 11, 1985, p. AA 4.

Currently, there is a great disparity between the vulnerability of Soviet and Western governments. The latter are risking their lives every day; attempts on the lives of American presidents, the Pope, and the British prime minister show this very persuasively. If amateurish terrorists and psychopaths can shoot the president or the Pope in the middle of the day, it does not take much imagination to think what a group of professionals could do with money, logistical support, and training. There are several thousand East Bloc agents planted in the United States alone; with all the weapons and technology available to them on the spot, a coordinated one-shot terrorist volley could have a devastating effect. A great danger for the open societies also lies in the fact that 70 percent of all communications in the United States travel via satellites. This means that communication links are vulnerable to tampering and disinformation. If equipment for conducting such operations is affordable for individuals, it is certainly affordable for the Soviets. Most of the required equipment could be freely purchased in the West.

Openness, both the blessing and the Achilles' heel of Western societies, is something the leaders of Western states are used to living with. For the Soviet leadership, however, openness means vulnerability, and vulnerability means weakness—something the enemy seeks to discover and exploit. As characterized by former Soviet Foreign Minister Andrei Gromyko in May 1985, "thousands of small and large telescopes are directed at us, looking for a sign of cracks." The Soviet technique of intimidation and bluff is based on the Party's belief that the most vulnerable point of the West is its attachment to bourgeois *Nezhnichanie* (endearments) and its respect for human life, which paralyzes the West every time a confrontational situation occurs. This gives the party its greatest psychological and strategic advantage.

The ability and readiness of the Party to sacrifice as many lives (of ordinary people) as is necessary was once again demonstrated during the Chernobyl nuclear disaster. Tens of millions of people were exposed to radiation during the May Day celebrations, for exclusively ideological purposes. By then, the leadership was fully aware of the scope and danger of the disaster; yet it chose to herd people into the streets. This ability and readiness to jeopardize and sacrifice the lives of its own people gives the Party a much stronger position in each and every conflict with the West, and allows it to press its case far more aggressively than any Western government could afford to do.

If, however, the United States—and perhaps other countries—develop the capability to threaten the Soviet leadership, the Party will lose its greatest source of strength. The Party's performance in the Second World War, when the elite virtually fled Moscow in October 1941; their record in the war in Afghanistan, which their children evade; their escape from Chernobyl (documented in the emigre magazine *Posev* No. 6, 1986); these and other examples show that the Party elite is far less courageous when it comes to personal sacrifice than its Western counterparts. This feature of the Soviet elite's mentality suggests that, under the threat of a direct surgical strike, the Party would be much more inclined to compromise, renounce its missionary drive, and accept genuine political coexistence.

3.
The Technological and Economic Ramifications of SDI

In order to evaluate correctly the possible ramifications of the SDI program for the economies of the Soviet Union and the United States, we must understand that it is only part of a much larger technological revolution. Thus, we must begin by analyzing the nature of this revolution. In addition, we must also examine the differences between the previous and current stages of the arms race.

The Current Technological Revolution

Technical Aspects of SDI

Ever since ballistic missiles were invented, scientists and engineers have searched for ways to counter against them. In and of itself, a missile is an extraordinarly fragile thing. It is loaded with highly flammable fuel, explosives, sensitive electronic devices, a delicate guidance mechanism, and so on. It has a very thin shell, and its nuclear explosive can be detonated only by the precise sequence of a number of events. There are thus a great many ways to destroy or cripple a ballistic missile.

What makes the nuclear missile such a formidable weapon is its relatively small size and, primarily, its very high speed—about twenty times faster than a bullet. Therefore, the challenge in devising countermeasures lies in locating and tracking the missile, rather than in destroying it. This latter task can be done by a variety of means: ordinary explosives, a laser beam, an elementary particle beam, a nuclear explosion, microwaves, or mechanical impact. The rocket could also be misled on an inaccurate course, or even destroy itself if it receives a wrong signal.

In order to locate a ballistic missile, however, one has to detect its launch promptly; identify its destination; calculate the rocket's speed (that is, "freeze it in space and time"); make a decision which weapon to use; orient the weapon; shoot; verify its destruction; and, if necessary, shoot again. All this has to be done in a matter of minutes. The fact that any system must perform these tasks simultaneously against hundreds of missiles and the countermeasures of the enemy make the anti-ballistic missile task formidable indeed. Obviously, no human being could hope to accomplish it without the help of computers and robots. Our senses are too limited, and we think and talk too slowly. For example, it takes a fighter pilot approximately twelve seconds to identify a target, while a computer based on very high speed integrated circuits (VHSIC) can complete this task in three one-hundredths of a second—in complete darkness. Both Soviet and American scientists have been searching for ways to destroy nuclear missiles for four decades.[53] However, only after the invention of compact and powerful integrated circuits in the 1970s—making possible a rate of calculation thousand of times faster than before—did the identification, tracking, and destruction of ballistic missiles become theoretically possible without resorting to nuclear explosions.

Several features of future ballistic missile defense make it completely different from all previous defensive systems, including tanks, aircraft, battleships, and nuclear weapons. First and foremost, SDI, as conceived by the United States, is fundamentally a defensive system. It would not threaten anybody, and would not be activated until a missile is launched in the direction of the United States or its allies. SDI is thus similar in purpose and function to antiaircraft artillery—hardly an offensive system. Of course, one can argue that protecting a country increases its offensive capabilities; if so, raising a fence around one's house would also be categorized as an offensive measure.

Secondly, SDI is designed, so to speak, to correct a historical mistake made by mankind: the invention of a weapon of self-destruction before having achieved general adherence to peaceful methods of conflict resolution among nations. In a world where struggle—be it military, economic, or political—is considered by some countries to be their *raison d'etre*, rendering nuclear weapons obsolete (or at least impractical) seems a prudent thing to do.

Thirdly, the technologies required for a BMD system are such that they would find a wide variety of applications in nonmilitary areas. Some have argued, for example, that we do not need lasers capable of drilling holes at a distance of several thousand miles, or precision-guided munitions. This is not true. The latter system is nothing but a robot, guided by sensors and high-speed processors; everyone acknowledges the usefulness of robots. Directed energy sources could also be used for many other purposes. They may prove capable of providing large, orbital space stations with energy from the ground—or, conversely, for collecting energy in space and transmitting it to earth. Moreover, the principal problems standing in the way of achieving an effective BMD system—essentially the challenge of man-

[53] *English-Russian Dictionary of Air and Antiballistic Missiles Defense Terms*, published in Moscow in 1961.

aging very complicated, fully automated systems—are the same problems U.S. industry must solve in meeting the growing competition from low-labor cost foreign producers. More than any other program of the past, SDI promises great rewards for mankind, both technological and psychological.

The General Technical Requirements of SDI

Many of the technological challenges faced by the economy and society as a whole are addressed by the requirements any future BMD system must satisfy. A BMD system must be global, highly automated, and at least partially located in space. Thus, a number of requirements can be deduced. First, constructing such a system will depend on the ability to build a truly global command, control, communication and intelligence (C^3I) network. All the elements of this system should be able to communicate with each other in "real time." Therefore, human participation must be reduced to the absolute minimum, and most of the task allocated to robots. To coordinate them, correct the inevitable mistakes, and quickly adapt the entire system to the changing circumstances of a real battle, will be impossible without artificial intelligence.

Because one has no choice but to combat missiles where they fly, many elements of a BMD system must be placed in space. Therefore, they have to be as compact and light as possible. This makes miniaturization one of the most prominent and crucial tasks. Additionally, the entire system will still weigh perhaps several thousand tons, and will need maintenance and refueling. New, cheaper ways to fly in space, such as aerospace jets, will thus need to be developed. Finally, the system will have to be able to destroy missiles thousands of miles away in seconds. It therefore must include weapons that utilize directed and highly concentrated beams of energy, or superfast kinetic energy weapons.

These construction requirements for a BMD system combine to make the current stage of arms race different from previous ones. The two basic features of SDI are that:

- It is not a particular weapon, nor can it be based on just one or a few technologies. Instead, it requires the simultaneous development of many technologies.
- It essentially represents a qualitative—not quantitative—leap forward in the technological revolution.

Compared to the complexity and variety of tasks presented by SDI, the nuclear bomb program was very simple. In fact, dozens of countries could today build nuclear weapons. They choose not to build them for various reasons, but mostly because their main enemies usually live so close to them that the usage of nuclear weapons seems rather dangerous and impractical. The challenges of building rockets are far more formidable and involve the whole range of technologies: chemistry, guidance and communications systems. Yet, the basic technology is forty-five years old and has not changed significantly since the Germans mastered it—following which they manufactured and launched 1,115 V-2 rockets.[54] In contrast, BMD requires the development of a whole constellation of technologies, each one of which might spawn many other technologies. None of them can be developed on their own, and none of them is a single technology in and of itself. They are intertwined, they complement each other; each of them is equally vital to the competitiveness of the nation's economy. This leads to very stringent demands on the economy, infrastructure, social relations, and educational standards of any nation determined to undertake such an endeavor.

The Role of Computers

Electronics, and computers in particular, occupy a key place in the SDI program. Practically every single element of a future BMD system will incorporate some kind of microprocessor (chips). Mechanical devices, even electric components, will be replaced or radically transformed by customized chips. Generally speaking, computers and sensors will give inanimate devices the ability to sense, to think, and to talk to each other and to humans. Moreover, computers themselves will become intelligent, i.e., acquire the ability to learn and understand our language, accumulate knowledge and even acquire "common sense." When this happens, the mental power at our disposal will increase thousands of times.

Artificial intelligence is crucial for an essentially leak-proof BMD system. In the same sense, the competitiveness of the nation depends, in large part, on its mental capacity and its ability to handle enormous amounts of information. It is important to realize, however, that computing is not a single technology. It is rather a concept based on, and dependent upon, many technologies.

New Materials

New materials are next in overall importance. Only recently has mankind begun to use materials that do not exist in nature. Yet, we still make these materials "by trial and error." We randomly bring together many different elements, subject them to special physical conditions—extreme temperature, pressure, weightlessness—and see what happens. Sometimes this results

[54] James L. Stokesbury, *A Short History of Air Power* (New York: William Morrow, 1986), p. 234.

in curious new materials, for which we then try to find some use. We have happened upon many interesting materials this way, but these discoveries remain largely a matter of luck.

Metal-martix, carbon-carbon, and ceramic composites have already created a whole new range of possibilities. However, a true revolution in new materials is only now appearing on the horizon. The future in this area certainly belongs to so-called "nanoscience," which promises us the ability to design materials with predetermined qualities. New materials, particularly those that are light, strong and temperature-resistant, are essential for the success of SDI. At the same time, improved methods of creating new materials will expand enormously the ways to design and manufacture materials for consumer goods. The competitiveness of the American economy in the future will depend very heavily on our ability to master the technology of creating materials with predetermined qualities.

Sensors

The BMD system will depend on sensors sensitive enough to "see, hear and feel" at great distances, in darkness, through clouds, smoke, and perhaps even beneath the ground. They also have to be compact enough to fit into rockets. This requires the development of a whole range of electro-optical technologies. At the same time, sensors could have an enormous number of applications for consumer goods. When consumer goods acquire the ability to remember, see, recognize their master and other objects, the time of the "dumb" objects that now surround us will soon end. It is extremely important for Americans to be on the cutting edge of the technology of compact and clever sensors. The creation of an automobile "autopilot" system, for example, depends entirely on sensors; so do more efficient traffic control systems.

These are only a few of the technologies essential or critical for the success of the SDI program. In the words of Malcolm W. Browne, "For better or worse, these new technologies seem destined to change the world."[55] Technology itself is inherently neutral—that is, it can be used for both good and evil. It is the creators of technology—mankind—who are ultimately responsible for the purposes ultimately chosen. The most effective way of suppressing the evil use of technologies has thus far been openness. An evil application of technology presupposes a degree of monopoly over pertinent information. The current technological revolution, however, is essentially an informational revolution. It is thus inherently hostile to any monopolistic control over information or knowledge. Indeed, the very essence of this revolution lies in the facilitation of communication among people, and the

[55] Malcolm W. Browne, "The Star Wars Spinoff," *New York Times Magazine*, August 24, 1986.

increase of their personal intellectual capabilities. The fact that these technologies could also eliminate the greatest threat to mankind makes it difficult to see how they could change the world for the worse.

One thing is clear, however—this technological revolution imposes strict demands on the economies of both superpowers. Which of the two socio-economic systems is better equipped to face the challenges of the new technological revolution? Will the ability to concentrate effort and resources on specific technologies, as well as the Party's determination to succeed, prove a decisive advantage for the Soviets in the long run? Will the new technological race bleed the Soviet economy white, or invigorate it? Will the American economy be crippled by the military burden imposed by SDI, or benefit from it? To answer these questions we have to look at what the SDI program demands from the economies of both superpowers.

The Major Demands on the Economy

The creation of compact yet powerful computers requires the development of a whole spectrum of new technologies: new materials, new instruments, automated methods of control and production, computer-aided design, engineering, and manufacturing. Packing thousands of transistors into an area equal to the diameter of a human hair requires equipment and production methods that are typically found today only in scientific research. The technology of new materials with predetermined qualities is, in turn, dependent on artificial intelligence, tunable lasers, X-ray microscopes, new manufacturing methods, new instruments, and so on. The creation of an aerospace plane would require new materials, supercomputers, computer-aided engineering and manufacturing, new navigation systems, and so on.

These and many other areas of the technological revolution now underway are all intertwined, and stimulate each other to such an extent that failing to develop one area will retard development in others. To push all of them at once is, of course, a colossal task, impossible without the proper infrastructure, industrial base, educational base, and perhaps new forms of motivation. If industry is to incorporate some of the methods of science, it surely will have to incorporate some of the motivations that drive scientific research. These are much more complicated than simply financial success. Scientists are driven more by the prospect of acquiring power of knowledge and intellectual influence than by the prospect of financial reward. A sense of contributing to resolving the deadly dilemma created by nuclear weapons can be also a powerful stimulant to the creativity of scientists and engineers. Powerful creative forces can be generated by a sense of historical mission and responsibility. With due respect to the enormous stimulating potential of market forces, they alone cannot provide this sense of mission. Yet, this enormous reserve of creativity must not go untapped. The government, and only the government, can give scientists a sense of important national mission.

In this regard, the problems faced by the Soviet and U.S. governments are quite different. The Soviet government constantly appeals to the scientists' sense of duty and responsibility toward the motherland. However, since the end of the 1960s—when about one thousand of the best Soviet scientists called on the government to institute democratic reforms and were brutally harassed in response—the gap between the scientific community and the government has become unbridgable. The fate of Andrei Sakharov—one of the finest scientists and the conscience of the Soviet scientific community—remains a source of mistrust and even hostility between the Party and the scientists, despite his recent release from internal exile. Therefore, it is very hard to imagine that the Soviet scientific community will be sparked, as at the end of the 1950s, by the government's appeal to patriotic feelings and their sense of mission.

The U.S. government faces a similar problem with the "concerned scientists" who are anti-SDI. However, this group represents a relatively small portion of the American scientific community. In addition, the gap between them and their government is not as great as is the case in the Soviet Union, because it originates in misunderstanding rather than deep hostility. The "concerned scientists' " position is emotional to such an extent that it occasionally works against their own interests. They try to generate guilt among their colleagues for participating in research work that promises perhaps more to basic science itself than to the military. They also omit from their calculations the fact that government can effectively stimulate the huge reserves of the American industrial complex at very little cost to the taxpayers. This stimulation is particularly rewarding during the research stage. Yet, curiously enough, the "concerned scientists" recently initiated a campaign to curb funding of SDI-related research.

The Future of American Industry

At a time when the American economy is suffering from low-labor-cost foreign competition, technology offers it a second chance. We are moving toward a world of customized goods. Perhaps ten or twenty years from now, there will be three types of markets: basic goods, produced by the millions in huge, highly automated factories; semicustomized goods, derived from basic goods by the addition of a variety of optional features; and fully customized goods, produced from scratch according to customers' special requirements.

Wealthy societies will obviously form the largest market for customized products, and their industries are best positioned to satisfy these markets.

Eventually the customer may come to a company, talk to a design engineer and financial expert, and a couple of weeks later drive away a unique car at a price hardly above that of today's regular car. Computer-aided design, engineering, and manufacturing will make possible the production of uniquely designed custom goods on a mass scale. Service and manufacturing functions will merge, promising new life to American industry and giving new meaning to the service branches of the economy. As it stands now, services have grown at almost an appalling pace, while the manufacturing sector has been shrinking.

Edward Luttwak remarked recently that America is heading toward a future when it will be a nation of clerks and hotel managers, in which Japanese tourists will stay. However, a potentially huge American market for customized goods offers a solution to this danger. Of course, American industry has to resolve many technological problems. Interestingly enough, however, these are the same problems with which SDI is concerned. J. Tracy O'Rourke, the president of Allen-Bradley, has stated: "The success of tomorrow's industrial plant will depend on its ability to gather, share, and utilize information for more productive planning and control."[56] This is precisely one of the main problems that creators of a BMD system must solve. Therefore, it is only reasonable that industry and the SDI program stimulate and aid each other.

The Technological Challenge Facing the Soviet Economy

While the United States needs first and foremost to gain the commitment of its politicians and scientists and improve its educational base, the Soviet economy and scientific-technological institutions confront very different problems. The nature of these problems has to be understood in order to assess correctly the ramifications of SDI for the Soviet economy and society in general.

The Soviet leadership suffers from no lack of commitment; the country has an impressive pool of scientists, engineers, and research institutions. It has tremendous resources and the ability to manipulate them. Yet the problems of the Soviet leadership are much deeper than those of the United States. The Soviet economy once was like putty in the fingers of Soviet leaders. Now this putty has become so fluid that economic power is slipping through the Party's hands. There are several unavoidable facts which deeply worry the Party.

[56] Jeffrey Bairstow, "GM's Automation Protocol," *High Technology*, October 1986.

Physical Dimensions of the Two Economies

An emphasis on both absolute and relative economic growth in the socialist bloc has always been the backbone of Soviet propaganda. "I grow, therefore I am real and alive:" one cannot overestimate the importance of this assertion for the survival of the Soviet myth. With every passing year, however, the Party finds it increasingly difficult to maintain this idea. For some time now, the relative size of the Soviet bloc, from both a demographic and an economic point of view, has ceased to expand.

However, the U.S. economy has been growing relatively larger. As Zbigniew Brzezinski has written: "In 1950, the Soviet GNP accounted for about 11 percent of the world economy; three decades later it still constitutes 11 percent."[57]

Since the 1920s, the U.S. economy has been the main target of Soviet propaganda. Moscow has always emphasized the much faster growth of the Soviet economy compared to the United States. However, even official Soviet data draw a different picture; the Soviet GNP was only 54 percent of U.S. GNP in 1976, and only 51 percent in 1985.[58] Given inflation, and the fact that production of such important components of the Soviet GNP as oil, steel, coal, and agriculture (among others) has fallen during the last three years to below 1980 levels, it is possible that the second largest economy in the world is not the Soviet, but the Japanese.

Official Soviet data show an average of 2.8 percent annual growth in GNP during the last five years. Even if we accept these questionable data, actual growth—taking into account perhaps two percent annual inflation—is less than one percent, and perhaps closer to zero. (Some Western observers think that the per capita growth of Soviet economy stopped as early as 1978.)[59] In contrast, the U.S. economy showed 2.7 percent average annual growth during the last decade, and its workforce expanded by fifteen million people—more than the entire labor force of Spain. Both of these tendencies have become even more pronounced during the last three years. In recent years, the Soviet labor force has been growing by less than 500,000 annually, while the U.S. labor force has grown by three million per year. If the Soviet economy is indeed shrinking in size relative to the U.S. economy, one of the main claims of the Party's myth has been proven false: "The wave of

[57] Zbigniew Brzezinski, *Game Plan* (New York: The Atlantic Monthly Press, 1986), p. 124.

[58] The author's calculations are based on Soviet data on GNP in 1976 and its growth since then. See: *Norodnoe Khoziaistvo SSSR* (Moscow: Statistika, 1977), p. 98.

[59] See Michael Ellman, "Did Soviet Economic Growth End in 1978?" in Jan Drewnowski, ed. *Crisis in the East European Economy: The Spread of the Polish Disease* (New York: St. Martin's Press, 1982), pp. 131-142. Also Alexander Nove, "Has Soviet Growth Ceased?" *Manchester Statistical Society* (Manchester, England: November 15, 1983), p. 24.

history is on our side." It is only a matter of time before this fact becomes universally accepted.

The Technological Gap

Another worry for the Soviet leadership is the increasing technological gap between the two countries. During the last decade, U.S. investment in research and development has been growing at more than 9 percent annually, whereas Soviet investment has grown by only 3.5 percent annually. One unidentified Soviet scientist has said:

> What really worries our leadership about America's space-based defense is not the new military capability. It is the effort to rally Western Europe and Japan into a high-tech research alliance with America that will condemn Russia to permanent mediocrity.[60]

From the very beginning of the Soviet era in Russia, official literature has emphasized the importance of scientific-technological progress. Sometimes Soviet leaders have sounded truly apocalyptic: "We are fifty or a hundred years behind the leading countries [technologically]. We must make up this distance in ten years. Either we do it, or we shall perish."[61] Although Stalin's statement was a bit too dramatic, Soviet officialdom has never stopped repeating the theme. Consider the views of a leading Soviet military expert, writing forty years after Stalin:

> The contemporary scientific-technical revolution is one of the main sectors of the historic competition between capitalism and socialism. An important field for the active use of its achievements, therefore, is the armed defense of our country and the entire socialist commonwealth.[62]

There is little doubt that Soviet scientists and military experts, considering all the potential spinoffs of the new technological race triggered by SDI, understand that the Soviet Union may increasingly become an underdeveloped country from an economic and technological point of view. Loren R. Graham, a professor at the Massachusetts Institute of Technology and a long-time student of Soviet science, has said of the Soviet scientific community: "They realize that, if they do not make significant advances soon, they will be left permanently behind in key areas."[63]

A document recently smuggled out of the Soviet Union, which clearly originated in the elite circles, indicates an awareness on the part of at least

[60] *U.S. News & World Report,* March 3, 1986.

[61] Stalin, February 4, 1931 *Sochinenia* (Moscow: *Politizdat,* 1951) vol. XIII, p. 39.

[62] Colonel V. Bondarenko, *Kommunist Vooruzhennykh Sil,* No. 24, December 1971, p. 9.

[63] *U.S. News & World Report,* October 1, 1984.

one segment of the Soviet elite of the danger posed by the growing technological gap between the Soviet Union and the West.[64] Marshal Ogarkov's own pronouncements reinforce this view.

Competition in Conventional Weapons

It is true that the Soviet economy generates only 2.5 percent of international trade. This trade, however, is large enough for limited competition in at least three areas: consumer goods on the domestic market; and, in the international market, raw materials and military hardware. In these three areas, only Soviet raw materials compete successfully on the international market. Soviet military hardware has found a market niche in those Third World countries quarrelling among themselves that do not need—or cannot afford—expensive and sophisticated Western equipment. Outside these countries, Soviet military hardware cannot compete with the products of the capitalist countries. Although failure in this competition would not entail economic bankruptcy for the Soviet Union, it might have a considerable and cumulative impact on its ideological standing. It might also have a deleterious affect on its hard currency earnings which, in turn, would affect its ability to purchase Western technology and grain.

The American retaliatory strike on Libya of April 1986 clearly showed, once again, that the quality of today's weapons is largely measured by their ability to conduct electronic warfare. "What you stuff into a helicopter or aircraft used to be minor," says one industry executive. "Now the electronics and avionics dominate. Electronics account for 50% of the cost of some of today's combat aircraft."[65] In other words, though two aircraft might look alike, even having similar external characteristics (speed, range, size, cruising altitude, and so on), yet one may be able to see, sense, calculate, and shoot at, from any position, many targets at once and at a far greater distance—and be practically invisible on the other's radar screen. Being inferior in these respects would make a plane completely helpless and useless.

Countries with recent first-hand combat experience—Egypt, Syria, Iraq, Libya, and Iran—know that Soviet military hardware is no match for its Western equivalent. (This could be a reason for the reduction of Soviet military sales to these countries in recent years.) The Soviet Union is currently losing the arms race in those areas where electronics and new materials are crucial. If this tendency continues—and the Soviet Union falls farther behind the West in conventional military technology—the Party will continue to lose leverage over countries "fighting for their national liberation." The

---

[64] "Soviet Freedom Manifesto," *Washington Times*, July 23, 1986, p. 1A. A full version of it was published in *Posev*, No. 9, 1986.

[65] *Business Week*, July 28, 1986, p. 31.

poor international reputation of its military equipment is undermining another pillar of the Soviet myth: "The socialist socioeconomic system is more efficient and more productive, and the future belongs to it." The growing disparity between the quality of Western military hardware and that of the Soviets might eventually convince Third World countries that being allied to the Soviet Union automatically means being on the losing side. By now they have learned that the Soviets are hardly capable of providing essential economic assistance. Moreover, as seen in the case of Ethiopia, it is not the Soviets who are likely to provide food—though people are starving by the millions.

Consumer Goods

Soviet consumer goods do not compete with Western goods on international markets; however, they do compete on the USSR's black market. Soviet consumer goods lost their reputation for quality among the educated classes of Soviet society long ago. The low regard for domestic goods is spreading very rapidly, so much so that the situation is becoming truly embarrassing to the Party.

It is a well known fact that in the Soviet black market any foreign consumer product costs three, four, sometimes ten times more than its domestic equivalent. The cheapest foreign goods are probably those of Polish and Bulgarian origin. The ratio follows a well established rule: The more capitalist the country from which a product comes, the bigger the difference between its price on the black market and that of a similar domestic product. The difference may sometimes be as large as one thousand percent, a difference both staggering and clearly unjustified—at least by considerations of quality alone. In the popular mind, the most capitalist country is of course the United States. Therefore, as a rule, American goods cost more than European or Japanese products, even though the quality of the latter might actually be higher. This rejection of domestic products is certainly rooted in more than economic considerations; it is a political statement as well. Only political and psychological motivations can help explain why anybody would pay the equivalent of a Soviet engineer's monthly salary for one pair of American blue jeans.

This phenomenon would be a curious but unimportant feature of Soviet social culture, were it not for the fact that the elite—and particularly their children—are the most vigorous promoters of this philosophy. Wearing capitalist clothing is something like belonging to a very exclusive club. Only a few can afford Japanese VCRs, Sony Walkmans, Swedish furniture and the like. These few belong to the highest layer of the elite. Their preferences testify better than anything else to the supremacy of the capitalist economic system.

The Question of Quality

The new information age is an age that demands close to absolute standards of quality. When manufacturing takes place at the molecular (and even atomic) level, accuracy and cleanliness become the very essence of the technological process. The workplace in a semiconductor plant, for example, has to be one thousand times cleaner than a hospital operating room (measured by the number of suspended air particles). Creating and maintaining a proper environment in these industrial facilities requires a tremendous amount of equipment and investment. For example, just the filtration and temperature control equipment for a small plant making run-of-the-mill semiconductors can cost more than $1 million.[66]

The future of American industry depends perhaps on its ability to switch to fully automated production methods and to orient itself toward customized products. However, new manufacturing methods are hardly possible within the framework of the social relationships currently prevalent in companies. They will require new relationships among the employees, management, designers, engineers, technicians, and supervisors. An adversarial relationship between any two of these groups will result in substandard quality. One angry or frustrated computer operator could disturb the technological process in such a way that the problem might remain undetected until after a great deal of harm had been done. Similarly, one slightly tipsy employee could throw the whole environment out of kilter. If relationships between employees and management of a plant are confrontational, the employees will be able to sabotage the production process so easily that management will be completely at their mercy. Fear of reprisals as a principal motivating factor works well in conditions where the volume of production is more important than quality, and where the quality of products can easily be controlled. But at a certain level of product complexity, when manufacture is based on thousands of interdependent operations, the number of parameters becomes too great and too illusive to be measured and enforced by fear alone. At this point, the quality control function, to be truly effective, must be located inside every operator. For that to occur, that individual must be genuinely interested in the process, and in the results of his work.

Finally, today's technological revolution requires a burst of creativity from millions of scientists, engineers, and manufacturers. These people have to be highly motivated. They must have the freedom to obtain any information they need, to talk to anybody, to have flexible work hours, and so on. In

[66] *Business Week*, June 10, 1985, p. 88.

sum, only a high quality of life can make possible the high productivity levels and creativity necessary in the new technological revolution. New levels of technology require a whole new physical and social environment. The difficult experience of many countries that have tried to import technology without having the requisite infrastructure and social culture shows that only limited success will be realized by such efforts. High technology and new manufacturing methods have an inner life and logic, which impose stringent demands on social culture. Either culture must eventually yield, or technological development will be retarded.

All this is equally applicable to Japan, Iran, the Soviet Union, and the United States. For the Soviet Union, however—where 51,000 men die annually of alcohol poisoning and many enterprises stop for a couple of days after paydays—the conflict between existing social culture and the requirements of high technology seem to be far more comprehensive than in the United States.

Of the many problems faced by the Soviet economy—its physical growth, productivity, discipline, level of investment and so on—the largest problem is, therefore, quality. As such, it presents the greatest stumbling block to the achievement of a Soviet SDI program.

Investment, by itself, has become less and less efficient as a means of resolving the problems of the Soviet economy—much less so than when the smokestack industries were being built. The most conspicuous evidence is the record of the agricultural and oil industries, which for many years have absorbed 55 percent of all Soviet investment. Between 1966 and 1980, the Soviet Union invested approximately 500 billion dollars in agriculture.[67] Yet, during that time, it moved from being a modest exporter of grain in the 1960s to the world's largest grain importer. In fact, the money invested could have bought all the grain they needed for ten years. Oil production has also flattened out, and even declined somewhat recently. In a striking statement, Soviet economists have said, in effect, that return on investment throughout the Soviet economy has reached a level so low that investment alone does not do much good.[68] The problems of the Soviet oil industry clearly indicate that unless an adequate infrastructure is constructed and the quality of life reaches a certain level, investments in equipment and even high salaries will not result in greater productivity. This was admitted by Mr. Gorbachev himself when he visited the oil production areas of western Siberia during the winter of 1985-1986.

The problem of quality is even more complex than the problem of productivity. Soviet officials have talked for over twenty years about quality as the number one problem. One of the latest complaints came from the

[67] *Sovetskaya Rossia*, January 23, 1983.

[68] See, for example, *Planovoe Khozaiistvo*, 1985, No. 2, and *Narodnoe Khozaiistvo*, 1984.

deputy chairman of Gosplan, Nikolai Lebedinsky: "Frankly, we have a problem with quality because of the lack of discipline in the use of technology and labor discipline."[69]

In the West, there is a widely accepted theory that Soviet military industry is capable of producing very high quality equipment because it is insulated from the rest of the Soviet economy and enjoys the highest priority and attention. This theory implies that the Soviet system can be effective if it is perfected. Some Western observers even suggest that, as a method of solving their problems, the Soviet leaders may try to emulate the experience of military industry in civilian sectors. This is a conspicuously erroneous theory; if accepted, it could lead us to very inaccurate conclusions about the potential of the Soviet economy.

The quality of Soviet military products is, indeed, considerably higher than that of consumer goods. This is primarily because there are probably twice as many controllers in military plants than in corresponding civilian ones. But the atmosphere and inner logic of military factories are exactly the same as one finds in the rest of the Soviet economy. Stealing and cheating, though less pervasive than in civilian factories, still flourish. In 1978, the author was approached in Kiev by a worker from the Arsenal Factory, which presumably produced air-to-surface missiles. This worker offered a beautiful ashtray made of a ruby-colored crystal for ten rubles. Not only had he stolen the materials; he had obviously been able to use the factory's equipment in making the ashtray, and then smuggled it out from his super-secret facility.

Doubling the number of controllers imposes substantially higher discipline, grounded in increased fear; but this obviously cannot change the basic fabric of relationships in military factories. Employees of such plants usually have better living conditions, kindergartens, food supply, recreational facilities, and so on. The relationships between the various layers of employees at both the military and civilian factories in the Soviet Union are purely adversarial. A "them vs. us" attitude characterizes relationships between each and every layer of the factory. Workers see themselves in opposition to everyone, starting with foremen. In their eyes, foremen and supervisors belong neither to the workers nor to management or engineer corps; yet they are still part of the same oppressive structure. A hostile and adversarial relationship also exists between managers and engineers. In the eyes of the engineers, the managerial staff is composed of failed engineers or know-nothing *apparatchiki*; they are nothing better than a parasite on the productive body of the factory.

Currently, the enforcement of quality and quantity control results from pressure by management on the engineer corps. Engineers, in their turn,

[69] *New York Times*, October 13, 1985.

pass along this pressure to the foremen and supervisers—who, in turn, pass it along to the workers. An increase in quality is thus possible only by increasing pressure, which, essentially, means increasing the level of fear. Of course, this only exacerbates the hostile, "us vs. them" relationships which already dominate factory life. The controllers are caught in this hidden battle. They are not independent; psychologically they belong to the engineers' camp, but have been placed as watchdogs over them. Administratively, they are not dependent on the managers, yet their financial security lies in the hands of the factory director and the Party chief. They are both a nuisance and a disadvantaged underdog, because nobody in the factory is genuinely interested in the quality of their products. Their main functions are to please everybody, and to be scapegoats when it comes to taking responsibility for poor quality. In the latter capacity, only the protection of the director can save them from severe punishment.

Thus the factory produces not for the consumers, but for the government. The government then sells the products to consumers either at home or abroad. As such, only the government is interested in quality. The factory's management is interested only in the quality it can get away with. Military representatives on the factory staff are independent from the regular factory management; thus they are more effective in enforcing quality control than controllers in civilian factories. However, they soon tend to "go native" and, in fact, conspire against the military. Finally, there is also a simple logistical reason why the enforcement of quality control by fear has its limits. The more complicated the production process becomes, and the more operations a product has to pass through—and hence the more controllers are needed. At some stage, the number of controllers approaches the number of workers and cannot grow any further.

The market, of course, presents a radical solution for the problem of quality. Both domestic and international markets provide, in the form of consumers, millions of controllers. These controllers, of course, are not professionals—but they do not have to be. If a product is of inferior quality, they do not care why: they simply do not buy it.

Reliance on Imported Technology

Among all the countries in the world, the Soviet Union is best positioned for large-scale production of basic goods—at least theoretically. The concentration found in Soviet industry is the highest in the world, and perhaps in human history. Two hundred Soviet factories, for example, produce fully 50 percent of Soviet industrial output. Hypothetically, with the help of Western technology the Soviet Union could flood the world with cheap basic products. In practical terms, however, the existing system makes this completely impossible.

In fact, the Soviet system is incompatible with Western technology. Although both the legal and illegal acquisition of Western equipment and technology is likely to intensify, this by itself cannot provide the Soviets with the ability to compete in the new technological race. In fact, if the current Soviet economic system persists, the effectiveness of acquired Western technology and equipment will decline over time. The reason for this is the growing complexity of contemporary technology. The Soviets have no choice but to rely on thousands of different producers of equipment, with accompanying thousands of different specifications. This also occurs in software; even the manuals are written in different languages. Sporadic espionage and black market purchases cannot satisfy indefinitely the requirements of Soviet industry. Paralyzing bottlenecks will inevitably ensue.

In fact, this problem already existed in Soviet research institutions in the late 1960s. A personal anecdote may help illustrate this point. In 1970 a good friend of the author received a contract from the biological department of Moscow State University to rebuild two American-made computers. Those who acquired them through Finland had failed to obtain two blocks that needed to be installed in order for the computers to be used for research purposes. Because this fellow was a uniquely gifted scientist specializing in electronics, he managed to rebuild these computers singlehandedly. It is unlikely, however, that it would be possible to perform such an operation on today's computers.

Problems of Infrastructure and Distribution

The totally centralized distribution of goods and services in the Soviet Union is an ingenious feature of the Soviet economic system. It will, however, prove one of the major stumbling blocks in moving toward the achievement of a comparable Soviet SDI program. This distribution system is responsible for the fact that consumers and producers do not have direct contact, but instead are separated by the government's intervening "Great Wall." The government learns about the need for particular goods and services primarily through citizens' complaints. Therefore, shortages and complaints are a vital mechanism of the Soviet planning process.

Centralized distribution leads to the creation of a centralized transportation and communication network. As a result, direct links between even closely located enterprises do not exist; the number of trucks available for direct deliveries is negligible; paved roads between enterprises practically do not exist; and, from a legal point of view, such direct deals are at least partially if not wholly illegal. Theoretically, any communication or business between any two enterprises must go through the central authorities. If the directors of enterprises followed this rule, however, none of them would be able to fulfill their production plan. Thus all break the law, and the government turns a blind eye to this practice for the sake of its own survival.

In fact, one can legitimately talk about a conspiracy between the government and the manufacturers against the consumers. The government establishes certain rules for factory managers, which it knows they will have to break. They do break them, but in return demand leniency from the government regarding the quality of their goods and the acquisition of certain material privileges. The government grants them these privileges and treats them mildly for the poor quality of the products, but in turn reserves the right to punish them for not fulfilling the plan. The loser in this game is obviously the consumer. His plight is chronicled in the official Soviet press, which is saturated with the most amazing and incredible facts. Here are only three examples:

> Nine out of ten television sets refuse to switch on while still on the store counters.[70]

> Last year, tests showed that combines "Kolos" and "Niva" [the latter is the model Soviets try to sell abroad] had an average working time before their first breakdown of 5.7 and 8.7 hours, respectively, while the international standard is 300 hours.[71]

> Prime Minister Nikolai Ryzhkov admitted recently that only twenty-nine percent of all manufactured goods in the Soviet Union correspond to Western standards.[72]

In fact, the actual number is much lower. Typically, those goods that receive the so-called Seal of Quality—supposedly given in recognition of their internationally high quality—cannot match Western products. The reason, as many Soviet publications have revealed, is that this medal can now easily be obtained through a widely accepted practice—namely, bribery.

The Soviet economy therefore faces several paramount problems with infrastructure, quality of life, productivity, creativity, and quality. Without a fundamental restructuring of the entire Soviet sociopolitical system, it seems the resolution of these problems will remain an unattainable goal.

[70] *Pravda*, April 26, 1985.
[71] *Sotsyalisticheskaya Industria*, October 1, 1982.
[72] *Washington Post*, June 19, 1986.

4.
Possible Soviet Responses to SDI

There are many uncertainties surrounding the possible Soviet responses to SDI. Will the Soviet Union increase its production of offensive weapons, or launch a preemptive strike when the United States starts actually to deploy its BMD? Will the Soviet leadership be ready to reduce dramatically its offensive weapons, believing them useless anyway? In order to compete with the United States in a new arms race, will the Soviet Union introduce market-oriented reforms—or further close its society and tighten discipline? Will the world be safer if the Soviet Union loses the technological race—and with it, its superpower status? And what should we do? Is it not better to leave things as they stand now, and instead try harder to find a political solution to this madness of nuclear confrontation?

The questions are endless, and perhaps there is no answer to many of them. The search for the answers to these questions, however, should be based on an understanding of how the Soviet political mentality translates into attitudes toward such significant factors as international treaties, arms development and deployment, technological progress and its impact on the Party's struggle, and so on. There are remarkable differences in the approaches taken by U.S. and Soviet political mentalities to these matters.

Perfectionism Versus Evolutionism

Consider, for example, how they differ in approaching the development and deployment of new weapons. The Soviet and U.S. approaches, respectively, could be characterized as "evolutionist" and "perfectionist." When American weapon designers decide to come out with a new product, they typically think in terms of state-of-the-art technology. (This "perfectionist" attitude apparently extends to society at large. In a study of 150 American salesmen with annual incomes ranging from $10,000 to $150,000, a psychologist, Dr. David Burns, discovered that roughly 40 percent of them proved to be perfectionists.)[73]

In Soviet social culture, perfectionism is completely missing. Perfectionists do exist—in a very small number—but judging from the ironic attitude and ill treatment they receive from the rest of society, they are regarded as

[73] *Psychology Today*, November 1980.

a strange species indeed. The Soviet mind is geared toward making things work *somehow* and dreaming about perfection. The Soviets believe that some kind of defense, no matter how imperfect, is better than no defense at all. The Soviet government thus procures whatever weapons systems it can, with the intention of upgrading them later and, in the meantime, having them "just in case." Anything useful—even if only marginally useful—is kept. Both the United States and the Soviet Union have been working on ballistic missile defense since the early 1960s.[74] The fact that the Soviet Union currently has a BMD system while the United States is trying to catch up—albeit on a much higher technical level—is an excellent illustration of the two mentalities at work.

The United States tried several BMD systems and scrapped all of them as insufficiently effective or efficient, with most criticism directed to the latter quality. The American contempt for technically inefficient solutions led indirectly to the ABM treaty—and to the fact that the United States now must play a catch-up game with the Soviets. In Soviet eyes, Americans—who throw away twenty-year old IBM typewriters because they want electronic ones, or stop production of the magnificent *Saturn V* booster because they prefer the state-of-the-art shuttle—are, in a word, insane. (Indeed, as the *Challenger* disaster showed, it would have been very handy to have had one or two dozen *Saturns* in reserve.)

By contrast, any Soviet laboratory or research institute working on defense-related matters will continue working, no matter how unproductive, on the belief that one day some breakthrough or bright personality will make a difference. Any rocket will be kept—even the oldest types, if they are still usable. ("Who knows, maybe one day somebody will find a good use for them, even if not for military purposes.") To Americans, it might seem strange—or even crazy—to accumulate "old junk." But from the Soviet point of view, the United States is equally crazy to scrap thousands of airplanes and tanks just because an immediate need for them no longer exists.

One can therefore be sure that the data on Soviet military hardware made available by the U.S. Defense Department in *Soviet Military Power*—and which some people find difficult to believe—in fact grossly underestimates the actual accumulation of twenty-, thirty-, or even forty-year old Soviet military equipment.

It is not that the Soviet approach should be emulated. However, it has at least one advantage. The technological revolution has brought new opportunities for modernizing and upgrading old hardware with new; for improving antiquated systems with more compact and efficient electronic equip-

[74] See, for example, William J. Broad, " 'Star Wars' Traced to Eisenhower Era," (*New York Times*, October 26, 1986.)

ment, motors, and guns; and so on. While the United States may redesign an entire weapons system from scratch—building a frame from composite materials, a new motor from ceramics, and taking ten to fifteen years in the process—the Soviets will take an old reliable frame and motor, add radar, infrared and laser guidance systems, and produce a quite effective weapon, even if not start-of-the-art.

Let us have a look at how the perfectionist and evolutionist approaches worked on two occasions. In the mid-1960s, the Soviets began deployment of a ballistic missile defense (BMD) system around Moscow. The Americans took several steps in a similar direction. By today's standards, the Soviet system was very crude and inefficient. It was primitive compared to the U.S. Nike-Zeus system—which had not been deployed—and less sophisticated than the Sentinel system, which was partially deployed, then suspended, by the Nixon Administration (and later dismantled). In 1975, the United States began deployment of Safeguard, a more sophisticated two-layered system. However, the next year it too was deactivated. Meanwhile, the Soviets were diligently improving their Galosh system, and spreading it throughout the European part of the Soviet Union. As a result, the Soviet Union now has a functioning BMD system which, even if not at the cutting edge, has been constantly upgraded and meticulously maintained. The U.S. has nothing comparable.

Similarly, the United States had an operational antisatellite (ASAT) system, consisting of ground-launched, nuclear-tipped missiles, as early as 1963. The technology was far from perfect: nuclear explosions tend to destroy or cripple satellites at great distances indiscriminately. So, in 1975, the U.S. government scrapped the system.

In the late 1960s, the Soviets also began testing an ASAT system, based on large SS-9 missiles with nonnuclear warheads. Because only half of the Soviets' twenty tests since 1968 were successful, some Americans—U.S. Air Force Chief of Staff General Allen among them—concluded that the Soviet ASAT system was not operational. The notion of what constitutes "operational" is thus another difference in Soviet and American mentalities. The perfectionist American typically sets requirements approaching 99 percent effectiveness, whereas the Soviets consider 50 percent effectiveness "good enough for the time being." In the future, they would reason, the system can be upgraded with better guidance systems, better conventional or even small nuclear explosives, and so on.

There is no doubt that the latest U.S. ASAT system, based on a "direct impact" weapon, is much more sophisticated than current Soviet ASAT weapons. However, even testing this weapon—to say nothing of deploying it—has become a bone of contention in the United States. The introduction of a dramatically new system is prone to appear an escalation of the arms race in the eyes of public opinion, while the gradual upgrading of existing systems usually goes unnoticed.

Cheating is also much easier to accomplish when one is upgrading an existing weapon. For example, it would be very hard—if not impossible—for the U.S. government to prove that the Soviets had equipped their ASAT system with small nuclear warheads, allowing a greater margin of error and thus a lower requirement for maneuvering capability.

The Party's Attitude Toward Treaties

Another important question is the extent to which treaties with the Soviet Union are helpful in restraining the arms race. An answer to this question requires an examination of Soviet and American perceptions of the very concept of a treaty. This is particularly important in light of the future prospects for the 1972 ABM Treaty.

Generally speaking, the fact of concluding a treaty is the manifestation of a lack of true trust. Good friends do not need treaties, just as lovers do not need government certificates. Their mutual trust and feelings are worth more than any piece of paper; no paper can save love or friendship when mutual feelings and trust dissipate. Thus, the United States has no arms control treaties with Britain or Canada; many agreements and accords, perhaps, but not arms control treaties. For the U.S. mentality, there is a logical contradiction, and some moral discomfort, in a written pledge to be a good friend.

Indeed, concluding treaties with an adversary presents the United States with a moral dilemma. In the American view, a treaty is a permanent solution, essentially a law. Therefore, Americans feel uneasy about breaking a treaty, just as they frown on breaking a law. They certainly do not contenance cheating, just as they do not tolerate scofflaws. On the other hand, the fact of entering into a treaty with a nation that does not share Western Judeo-Christian moral principles (such as, "thou shalt not lie") places Americans in the very discomforting situation of not being able to trust the other side. Americans tend to feel bad about themselves when they do not trust someone else, but in the case of the Soviet Union they have little choice.

The Soviet mentality holds a radically different attitude toward treaties with friends and enemies. The Soviet Union has numerous "treaties of friendship and cooperation" with a number of countries, which in itself is a very revealing fact. The Soviet political mentality, which precludes trusting anybody, least of all one's enemies, places a high premium on treaties with friends. A treaty of friendship between the Soviet Union and another state is considered to be a recognition of the existing hierarchy between them, and a written promise to respect it in the future. A long-term treaty with an actual or potential friend—a *true* treaty—is possible simply because coexistence is only possible with true friends.

No true coexistence with the enemy is possible, however; therefore, a treaty with an enemy has very different meaning and purpose. Lenin's teaching is as much a part of the Soviet political mentality today as it was sixty-five years ago:

> ...it is inconceivable for the Soviet Republic to exist alongside the imperialist states for long. One or the other must eventually triumph. And before the end comes there will have to be a series of frightful collisions between the Soviet Republic and the bourgeois states.[75]

As long as a true coexistence with the enemy is impossible, a treaty may prove a convenient way to restrain him. For the Soviet mentality, therefore, a treaty with an enemy is essentially a tactical maneuver—a sort of a truce, not an alternative to the struggle.

From the perspective of the Soviet mentality, one does not opt for a treaty when one is sure of victory. Warring sides resort to treaties when their struggle has reached an impasse, and both fear that continuing the struggle might lead to total defeat. Unlike a draw in chess, concluding a treaty with an enemy is only a suspension of the struggle, or of one of its specific forms. Moreover, a treaty with the enemy is a temporary compromise, and a compromise, of course, is an admission—indeed, a manifestation—of one's weakness. Therefore, from the Party's point of view, a compromise is permissible only as a tactical maneuver that will ultimately contribute to victory when *sootnoshenie sil* (a correlation of forces) permits. The correlation of forces does not cease to develop once a treaty is concluded; one must be prepared to take full advantage of it. One has to be flexible enough to shift emphasis from one form of struggle to another.[76]

In the mid-1970s, the Party decided that the correlation of forces between the socialist and capitalist systems had shifted decisively in favor of socialism. The U.S. failure in Vietnam, which resulted in the self-abnegation of the "Vietnam syndrome;" the Arab oil embargo and the resulting inflation, sluggishness in the U.S. economy, and stagnation in living standards; the humiliation of the President of the United States during the Watergate affair; and the overall weakening of U.S. international prestige, finally making possible the Iranian hostage crisis—all of this led, from the Party's

[75] V. I. Lenin, *Polnoie Sobranie Sochineniy*, v. 29 (Moscow: Progress Publishing House, 1965), p. 153.

[76] Natan Leites' analysis of these matters, in his book *A Study of Bolshevism* (Glencoe, Illinois: The Free Press, 1953) remains the single most important effort in this field. For a very instructive analysis of the Soviet attitude toward treaties with "imperialists" see Joseph D. Douglass, Jr., *Why the Soviets Violate Arms Control Treaties*, (Washington, D.C.: Pergamon-Brassey's, forthcoming 1987).

point of view, to a radical shift in the correlation of forces in favor of the socialist bloc.

The Soviet economy was growing by a respectable 3.5 percent annually; the Soviet Union had reached nuclear parity with the United States; and, in 1975, the borders of its domain were recognized de facto by the European nations as legitimate. The Soviet Union was partially protected by its BMD and nationwide air defense systems, and its leadership had an impressive chain of shelters. All this, perhaps, gave the Party a degree of confidence sufficient to undertake a series of strategic moves—most notably the invasion of Afghanistan, the backing of the Vietnamese invasion of Cambodia, and the consolidation of its grip in Angola and Ethiopia.[77]

As the 1980s began the situation again shifted drastically, this time in favor of the United States. The Soviet Union entered a period of economic and political stagnation, agricultural failure, pervasive corruption, and leadership crises. These internal difficulties were aggravated by external problems—tensions in Poland, reversals in Afghanistan, and finally SDI. Under these circumstances, the Party has had to regroup. It has sought first to reinvigorate itself, and then the entire society, in an effort to accumulate new strength. It now needs a truce, a temporary compromise with the adversary. Thus, the Party will be eager to engage in negotiations and to conclude treaties.

Should the United States take up this opportunity? Perhaps; but at a minimum we must be fully aware of the reasons for which the Soviet Union now seeks an accommodation: (1) because it needs a breathing space, and (2) because it wants to hinder the U.S. SDI effort. If it were to achieve these purposes, and the correlation of forces were to shift again in its favor, the party would of course embark on a new offensive. This does not mean that the treaties the Soviets had signed would be renounced publicly, because this would likely harm the Soviet Union politically. Instead, the Party would just quietly begin to ignore them. The Soviet moral code specifically rejects "bourgeois morality" because "it serves the class of exploiters." Therefore, the Party does not suffer from any painful moral compunction in breaking treaties based on bourgeois morality and law. However, the party knows that publicizing its contempt for "bourgeois morality" would be politically damaging. Therefore, its pragmatic approach is to violate treaties but never to renounce them.

[77] In the view of the author the Soviets were also ready to invade Iran in 1980. As I wrote in the French magazine *Le Point* in February 1980, the ultimate objective of the Soviet invasion of Afghanistan was Iranian oil fields. As American intelligence has now disclosed, the Soviets indeed amassed 350,000 troops on the Iranian border in August 1980. Perhaps it was the unexpected emergence of the Polish Solidarity movement that saved the Ayatollah Khomeini.

Soviet Reserves and Potentials

An "intelligent guess" about the Soviet response to SDI also needs to take into account analyses of Soviet economic, scientific, and technological reserves and potentials. In general, Soviet industry always produces as much as it can. It does not have the 20 percent capacity reserves characteristic of U.S. industry. Therefore, Soviet weapons production is already at its maximum level. This, however, does not mean that the Soviets do not have industrial or other reserves. They do have reserves—and those reserves are enormous—but they are very different from the reserves of U.S. industry and society in general.

Scientific and Technological Reserves

Although the Soviet Union has scored several "firsts" in weapons design, the general tendency since the Second World War has been for Soviet weapons designers to emulate Western innovations in military technology. When in 1967 about 30 percent of Moscow's university students went to work in "boxes"—which is how one refers to military research institutions—they were surprised and humiliated by the kind of job they were typically asked to do. Generally, they were given piles of Western technical documentation, mostly from the United States, to read and absorb for several months. They were then asked to duplicate this or that Western piece of military equipment. All the students were devoted admirers of Western technology; however, after immersing themselves in the details of design, they sometimes suggested different solutions to particular technical problems. All these suggestions were turned down. Every improvement in design involved so many changes in the technological process, so much trouble for so many people, that those who were particularly innovative were eventually forbidden from so much as talking about deviations from the original design. Needless to say, most of the students became so disillusioned and frustrated by their experience that they became desperate to leave their "boxes" and move to the financially less rewarding but much more loosely structured research institutions of the Academy of Sciences. In short, the research and design potentials of the Soviet Union are enormous, but the stifling effects of the system are even greater.

The Scientific Base

It is widely accepted among former Soviet scientists who now work in the United States that Soviet higher education, particularly in physics and mathematics, is superior to American education. The Soviet Union has 1.5 million scientists and engineers engaged in research and development in

1,500 research institutions. It has the world's highest commitment to research and development expenditures expressed as a percentage of GNP—3.7 percent—and yet, in the words of Soviet affairs analyst Thane Gustafson:

> By any measure—whether Nobel prizes, frequency of citation by fellow specialists, origin of major breakthroughs, or simply quantity of publications—U.S. scientists lead their Soviet colleagues in most disciplines, and in many there is simply no competition.[78]

Ph.D. candidates work very hard only during the three to five years of their programs. Once they earn their degree and occupy a cozy position, the overwhelming majority of them more or less cease to be active scientists. Their enthusiasm, however, can be relatively easily sparked. In 1966, while working on a master's dissertation, the author was approached by a friend who told me that he was looking for talented young scientists for part-time work on an exciting project. It happened to be a contract for the Ministry of Defense, although we were never told its purpose. My friend collected a group of twenty scientists, among whom I was perhaps the youngest. He outlined an exciting and appealing project: we were to find a way of registering extremely short electrical impulses. We would meet twice a month and write papers in our free time. Apart from that, we did not have any obligations and were offered very good money. These were the most productive nine months of my scientific career. We were very enthusiastic and creative, given such unheard-of freedom. After nine months, however, the project was shut down, because some official somewhere thought this kind of enterprise violated socialist law.

Our work had advanced relatively quickly, in part because it was still in the theoretical stage. It would have certainly slowed dramatically if we had moved into designing the instrument. This relative tempo is characteristic of Soviet science in general. Soviet science does relatively well during the "blackboard" stage, but starts stumbling once it moves into the experimental phase. Things become endlessly complicated at this stage, due to the lack of equipment, computers, technical support, and many other hurdles. Ph.D. candidates in experimental physics, for example, have been known to spend two out of the three years of their postgraduate program building experimental equipment, mostly with their own hands; then about six months conducting the experiment itself, and another six months writing their thesis. Those who had unlimited financial resources bribed the mechanics with vodka, and their dissertations consequently moved considerably faster.

In industry, I had the opportunity to work on an assembly line and as a technologist. The situation there is quite similar. Technologists do their best

[78] Thane Gustafson, "Why Doesn't Soviet Science Do Better Than It Does," in Linda L. Lubrano and Susan Gross Solomon, eds., *The Social Context of Soviet Science* (Boulder, Colorado: Westview Press, 1980), p. 31.

to design advanced processes for manufacturing various products, but at the manufacturing level only the most rudimentary of these instructions are followed. Perhaps 80 percent of the production process is constrained by the materials and equipment available. At the working level, the technology is determined by foremen, and it is "real" technology. The gap between paper technology and real technology is as large as the qualitative gap between Western and Soviet consumer goods. In sum, the inability to mass produce high quality industrial products is the main bottleneck of the Soviet economy.

Soviet Industrial Reserves

The Soviet economy similarly has tremendous reserves, but they are equally difficult to tap. Some of them are obvious, but enormous resources are concealed from the government, which can only speculate about their exact dimensions. Managers hide the productive capabilities of their factories from the government; if the government knew about them, it would immediately increase the factory's production quotas. By the same token, factory managers conceal their raw material supplies, equipment and spare parts stocks. If the government knew about these, it would immediately cut their supplies.

Calculations based on Soviet official sources suggest that the management of Soviet industry hides spare parts, raw materials and equipment worth as much as $200 billion from the government. My own experience as a technological engineer at a 500-employee factory in Kiev also leads me to believe that a typical factory could increase productivity by 25 percent without additional investments or structural changes, purely by additional motivation. This estimate coincides with official Soviet assessments.[79] If a lasting change in motivation occurred and was accompanied by the restructuring of management, the Soviet wage system, and relationships with suppliers, then the productivity of Soviet factories could perhaps double.

Soviet official data also show that the Soviet population maintains as much as $260 billion in official savings accounts. It is safe to guess that at least an equal amount of money has been accumulated in private hands and not reported publicly, because most illegal and semilegal profits from the rampant black market are naturally kept secret. The Party is mesmerized by the existence of these reserves, and since Stalin's death has tried to evolve a mechanism to tap them without once again resorting to mass terror. In this effort, however, the Party has been frustrated by the increasing complexity of economic life. This has forced it to tolerate black market activities

[79] See, for example: V. Parfenov, *Pravda*, May 20, 1985, and *Ekonomicheskoe Stroitelstvo*, No. 3, 1980, p. 51.

and grant more autonomy to factory directors. Hence, the researcher confronts a growing disparity between the data available to the government and the real data.

For example, Brezhnev's Food Program of 1982 allowed the directors of factories and enterprises to have auxiliary farms so that they could feed their employees. There are now about twenty thousand of these farms. This has certainly increased the hidden reserves at the disposal of these directors. A director, say, of a metal working factory in Krasnoyarsk, who may have a farm with five thousand hogs in the backyard of his facilities (an actual case), obviously does not report them to the Ministry of Agriculture. At the same time, his ministry is not particularly interested in hogs. Thus, the factory director is virtually free to manipulate this additional resource at will.

The disparity between the real picture and the data at the Soviet government's disposal could, in some cases, be as large as 50 percent. For example, when the government decided to build a chemical complex in Saratov in 1975, it was assured by experts that domestic industry could provide more than enough raw material to supply the complex. However, when the $130 million complex was completed three years later, the ministry discovered that domestic industry was able to provide only 30 to 40 percent of the necessary raw materials.[80] At least, in this particular case, this suggests the government had data about raw material production—and the capacity of Soviet railroads to deliver it—that was inflated by 60 to 70 percent.

As Seweryn Bialer notes, even high-ranking economists in the Soviet Union have little reliable data on the domestic economy:

> Every two years the Joint Economic Committee of the U.S. Congress produces a detailed overview of the Soviet economy written by the top American authorities within and outside the government. A high-ranking Soviet economist I spoke to found more, and more accurate, information in these volumes than in the meager data supplied him by the Soviet Planning Commission.[81]

One wonders how Western economists could possibly have more accurate data about the Soviet economy than that available to "high-ranking Soviet economists." Perhaps this is because of the two types of corrections to Soviet official data that they can make: they are better positioned to check records of Soviet international transactions with countries which do not withhold this data, and they can also correct for distortions in official Soviet data, which Soviet economists cannot do for political reasons. Thus, an American economist might say, for example, that Soviet data on GNP growth should be lowered by 2.5 percent due to inflation, whereas a Soviet economist

[80] *Sotsialisticheskaya Industriya* (Socialist Industry), February 2, 1983.

[81] Seweryn Bialer, *The Soviet Paradox* (New York: Alfred Knopf, 1986), p. 78.

would not be allowed to do this—because, officially, inflation does not exist in the Soviet Union, or exists only to a negligible extent. Surely, the Soviet economist knows much better than his U.S. colleague how the price of many staples has doubled, tripled, and even quadrupled since the end of the 1970s.[82] But he is not in a position to admit this fact openly, which would be tantamount to publicly accusing the Party of lying. These corrections, however, can only slightly improve the accuracy with which observers can assess the Soviet economic picture.

Altogether, the real economic picture remains a great mystery—not only to Western experts but to the Soviet leadership as well. It might well be that both Western observers and the Soviet government greatly underestimate the real economic resources of the Soviet Union. These resources, however, will remain essentially out of the reach of the Soviet government unless the present system shifts drastically toward a market economy.

The Limits of the Soviet Mentality

There is an obvious way to invigorate the Soviet society and economy—by introducing the market mechanism. The accumulated financial reserves in the hands of the population, together with the raw materials and spare parts the directors of factories have at their disposal, could ignite tremendous industrial activity. For this to occur, however, the factory managers would have to be allowed to produce directly for the market.

Perhaps this is what Mikhail Gorbachev had in mind in December 1984 when he told Robert Harley, a British Conservative Member of Parliament: "We want decentralization and market forces in industry, and the kind of technical innovation that exists in your ICI [a British chemical company]."[83] However, after September 1985, Gorbachev's initial promises of "dramatic, radical, revolutionary reform" shrank to talk about "further improvements of the planning mechanism."

For a market-oriented reform to become possible, the Party elite would have to yield voluntarily some of its power to the technocrats—particularly their power over scientific and production decisions—and would have to remove itself from the distribution process. This may not seem so difficult for people of a Western mentality. It would be an enormously difficult task for people who all their lives have operated on the basis of decrees and orders, substantiated by all forms of fear. For such a change to occur, the military would have to stop being the spoiled child of the society, taking

[82] See, for example, *Washington Post*, March 21, 1983; George Feifer, "Russian Disorders," *Harper's*, February, 1981; and Dmitry Mikheyev, "Might the Soviet Union Collapse?" *National Review*, May 1, 1981.

[83] *Sunday Times* (London), July 28, 1985.

whatever it wants. It would have to accept the position of one client bidding for the services of scientists, engineers, and manufacturers. The Party would have to abandon its role as the incontestable master and arbiter of the economy, assuming instead the role of mediator between different interest groups. While the Party might retain ultimate political power over society, it would certainly have to give up much of its status and prestige; the brightest, most active, and ambitious human beings would be funneled into industry, technology, and marketing. The Party would also have to share with the "technocrats" some of its dearest privileges: free access to information, to Western goods, to dachas, limousines, and trips abroad. Of these, access to information and to the West are the most crucial.

Furthermore, by yielding some of its monopoly on information, the Party would inadvertently create an independent public opinion. For example, an engineer or scientist who could get access to a computer and a printer would be sorely tempted to print a copy of a Solzhenitsyn book and sell it on the black market, where it would yield an amount equal to half of his monthly salary. Independent underground publications would appear in the hundreds. In fact, Polish dissidents claim that they are already "working on a program that will allow anyone with PC [personal computer] and laser printer to produce underground literature," so that, "[w]ithin a few years just about every engineer in [Poland] will be distributing uncensored information that way."[84] An independent mass media would emerge instantaneously, and the first thing it would question would be the legitimacy of the Party's rule—a situation quite unacceptable to the Party.

Moreover, the Party would have to follow the same rules and laws the rest of the society does, laws from which it currently exempts itself. As the brain and the nervous system of the nation, the Party is now above the law. It has its own Party code; only after this code has been applied and a person expelled from the Party is the civil law applied to him. With an independent public opinion, this double system could not survive for long.

People are captives of their mentality, and the Party leadership is no exception. Life remains for them a struggle for survival, a struggle between Them and Us; people are not to be trusted; strength is the ultimate argument; one can be only a master or a serf; the social structure is stable only when it is shaped as a pyramid; no form of power should be entrusted to individuals; the survival of the social structure is more important than one's personal survival; and to secure personal survival, one has to align one's activities as far as possible with the imperatives of the social organism. The Party must retain its position as the leader of socialist movement. It needs to maintain complete control over Soviet society, over other socialist states,

[84] Jackson Diehl, "Eastern Bloc's Pursuit of Technology Risks Upheaval," *Washington Post*, October 21, 1986.

and over its clients as well. This means that no disunity within the Party and society can be permitted. All key elements of political power—the secret police, the military, the economy, and information media—must be totally in the Party's hands. If the Party loses its revolutionary spirit and becomes corrupt, it must rid itself of its rotten elements, no matter how painful the amputation may be. New, vigorous, devoted people are always available. One needs only to place them in the right position.

SDI presents a formidable challenge—proving once again that "the enemy never sleeps," and is always searching for new opportunities to crush the Party. However, the Party has known far darker days: in 1919, for example, when the White Guards were very close to wiping out the first communist state, and in 1941, when Hitler was in Moscow's suburbs. At these times, the Party did not allow the technocrats to challenge its monopoly on power. Now, at a much safer time, it will not allow the imperialists to negate all the efforts it has made to build a magnificent military machine, second to none in the world.

In purely technical terms, the Party's leaders would find it very difficult to reorient themselves away from thinking in terms of millions of tons of oil and steel, billions of rubles, thousands of planes and tanks, which for them represent the real measures of power. It is very difficult for them to start thinking in terms of roads, telephones, bytes and bits, information services, and data banks accessible to all. It is very hard for them to imagine that quality, productivity and inventiveness cannot be achieved by discipline and closer supervision. It is hard for them to comprehend that in order to be able to compete successfully with the West in a new round of technological competition, they will have to decentralize their country's economic, scientific and transport systems—i.e., totally reverse the policy that they have been diligently pursuing for almost seven decades.

So what will the Party do?

Possible Soviet Responses

Mikhail Gorbachev addressed the issue of the Soviet response to SDI at a November, 1985 press conference in Geneva:

> The Soviet leadership has already given the relevant instructions to competent organizations and scientists and we can say that our response will be effective, less costly, and may be realized in a shorter period.[85]

This bravado only prompts a smile. If only it were true—it would be such a neat and simple way to resolve problems! However, there is little doubt

[85] *Foreign Broadcast Information Service*, (Soviet Union) December 10, 1985, pp. AA-16.

that the Soviet leadership will respond to SDI by undertaking some new actions, in addition to continuing what it has been doing all along, namely building up its military might as fast as possible.

Political Response

In times of trouble, the Party's attention always focuses first on itself. The thinking goes this way: If the Party is in trouble, there must have been something we did wrong, because the basics of our approach are right. So, what were our mistakes?

Obviously, it was wrong to allow old and inefficient members to remain beyond their time in the Politburo. Corruption also went too far, and has severely tarnished the reputation of the Party. Very vigorous cleansing has commenced, but more needs to be done.

Obviously, the economy was neglected and poorly managed. Technological innovations were not given proper attention. However, as always, the root of the problem must be sought in political matters. Here the main decisions are to be made. The Party should invigorate itself and initiate a political offensive, which will consist of two parts—overt and covert.

The overt response will consist of a number of attractive sounding proposals—in the arms control area, in peaceful cooperation, trade, cultural exchange, sport, science, and so on. New, energetic Party leaders will work out new proposals for Soviet-European space programs, oceanic or Antarctic exploration, grandiose East-West festivals targeted at West European youth, African or Asian conferences dedicated to life without conflict, and so on. The danger allegedly posed by the militarization of space, and on entrusting the fate of human civilization to computers, will be prominent topics at innumerable Soviet-sponsored forums.

On the covert side, the campaign to drive wedges between the West Europeans, Japanese, Chinese and Americans will start anew. The Soviets will again attempt to frighten Europeans by exploiting the Fortress America theme and by emphasizing their hostage-like situation. They will also be lured by the promise of cooperation in space exploration or in fusion reaction problems, which will be offered as alternatives to the militarization of space and the process of endangering the whole planet's existence.

The Party line will diligently ridicule the very concept of an impregnable shield over the West, in order to keep Westerners uncertain, afraid, and hesitant in their responses to Soviet military initiatives. They will do everything to postpone the deployment of U.S. BMD system in order to win time. We will see more and more Soviet "scientists" and experts on television, looking "just like us," speaking good English, talking about the danger and absurdity of the arms race, advocating cooperation and coexistence. We will hear new proposals from the Soviets to convene a "world conference for the peaceful use of the cosmos" and the like. If Americans and Europeans are reluctant to participate in these conferences, that will not reduce their political effectiveness; many countries, particularly the nonaligned nations, will be happy to do so.

We will probably see more Samantha Smith- or Jane Fonda-type envoys of both American and Russian origin travelling back and forth on "peace" missions.

At the same time, the Party might try to create new political troubles for the West without directly committing its own troops, advisors or large amounts of resources. This can be done by aggravating tensions at places which command a great deal of attention and energy in the West, in the United States particularly—Pakistan, Saudi Arabia, Mexico, South Africa, the Philippines. They are ripe for explosion, and hence a prime objective of the new breed of the Party professionals seeking to boost their careers. Therefore, we will see more Soviet diplomatic, trade, and cultural representatives in those countries.

Military Response

The military response will also occur on two levels. One will be geared to produce an immediate political effect; the other will be pursued over the long-term, and addressed to purely military concerns. The first of these will be relatively simple from a technological point of view, just enough to discredit, or at least shed doubts on, the very concept of SDI—that is, to have a desirable political effect. Efficiency, in this case, will be a secondary consideration, cost a tertiary concern.

The Party, in general, is rather reluctant to compete with the U.S. military-industrial-scientific complex on its playing field. In other words, as a rule the Soviets avoid overly complicated and sophisticated solutions; they prefer instead to rely on cunning and power to make up what they lack in quality and miniaturization. Therefore, as far as the military response to SDI is concerned, we may not see Soviet kinetic anti-missile weapons for a long time; but powerful microwave jamming transmitters, capable of disabling computers of the C^3I system (as well as those of battle stations and rockets) are very likely candidates. If a particular technology is perceived as rather inefficient from the U.S. point of view but simple from the Soviet perspective, the Soviets are likely to employ it. For example, if spinning a rocket, or warheads, can be easily done, the Soviets are very likely to take these measures. Even if they only increase the probability of penetration by 5 percent, this is equivalent to adding seventy rockets to the force of fourteen hundred that they already possess.

The Soviets are unlikely to increase dramatically their production of offensive weapons; they are already producing as many as they can. Tightening discipline can have a modestly positive short-term effect. But a dramatic increase in missile production would require restructuring many industries. The most recent five-year plan adopted in early 1986 indicates that no such boost in already high levels is planned. Generally speaking, the Soviets will be guided by the following principles: simplicity, power, impressiveness, and the availability of already existing technologies and equipment.

The list of potential options would include manned space battle stations equipped with powerful lasers; airborne chemical lasers; nuclear reentry vehicles (RVs) placed in space, and capable of reaching the earth's surface in minutes; powerful ground-based lasers able to blind or destroy U.S. RVs; further upgrading of their BMD system, and its extension to the entire European part of the USSR; nuclear artillery, perhaps even rail-gun nuclear artillery; nuclear sea mines; long-range ICBMs capable of reaching the United States via the South Pole; and space-based radio frequency jammers. These are not the suggestions of an expert on military technology, and the author might well be wrong in assessing the technical feasibility of these weapons. They are listed here simply to illustrate the general principles which might guide a Soviet military response.

At the same time, the Soviets will advance proposals on arms reductions that will be difficult to resist. For example, the Soviets might propose a dramatic reduction of the number of their troops in Eastern Europe, mostly from the German Democratic Republic. They may propose as much as a 90 percent reduction in offensive nuclear weapons in exchange for a ban on all BMD systems, and a comprehensive treaty on chemical and biological weapons. However, none of these treaties will call for the total elimination of these weapons.

Long-Term Technological Response

The Party is likely to concentrate on four or five basic technologies, and to build a corresponding number of scientific-industrial complexes from scratch—perhaps one for computers, one for materials, one for directed-energy weapons, and so on. A sign of this development appeared in *Literaturnaya Gazeta* in June 1986. It said that sixteen interbranch complexes have been already created, dealing with such issues as "technological lasers" and "biogen" (genetic engineering).[86] These complexes will probably be grouped in several new centers. The sites of the new complexes will likely not be located in Siberia or in the Far East, as in the past. The romanticism

[86] *Literaturnaya Gazeta*, June 20, 1986.

and the sense of a new era characteristic of the end of the 1950s cannot be revitalized. The new sites will probably be located in warm, civilized places that are relatively close to Moscow, and which have relatively developed infrastructure. Hence, the North Caucasus and the Crimea are strong candidates.

These will be gigantic centers, which combine research and production facilities. The Party will fill them with scientists in their thirties who would not have the chance in established laboratories and research institutes to advance their careers. East European and perhaps even Western scientists will be brought there; they will be provided with the highest living standards, including Western-made clothing, VCRs, cars, and so on. The Party will isolate such "bourgeois, decadent" places from the rest of the Soviet Union, giving them a flavor of exclusiveness and thereby attracting many scientists. These centers will have a fairly liberal political atmosphere: otherwise, the scientists would not abandon their cozy dissident circles in Moscow or Leningrad. All the production and research facilities will be equipped exclusively with Western equipment, including mechanized, automated production of chips and the like.

Only totally new centers can create the atmosphere of new possibilities and opportunities. However, the creation of three of these complexes will probably cost the Soviets dozens of billions of dollars. These centers will remain dependent on the rest of Soviet industry, which will therefore require at least some restructuring as well. This task will take at least ten years to accomplish—which is roughly the time the Party needs to delay the U.S. SDI program.

The Party is likely to intensify the courting and cultivation of small, nonaligned countries such as Austria and Finland, as well as developing countries like India and the Philippines, in order to use their research capabilities and gain access to U.S. and Japanese technology. They might build or sponsor factories in Singapore, Malaysia, or the Philippines, in order to copy the main components of U.S. and Japanese hardware for later assembly in the Soviet Union. Japan itself, with its very poor counter-espionage capabilities and open-door political climate, presents a great opportunity for the Soviets. To improve its chances in Japan, the Party might even return the Kuril Islands.

Illegal purchases of Western technology may acquire priority over acquisitions of technical documentation, particularly in the areas of artificial intelligence and computer-aided design. Rapid progress in these areas might bring the Soviets new solutions and options. For example, the theft of a Fairchild Instrument Corporation Xincom semi-conductor memory tester was a great success story for the Soviet Union. The unit can copy—that is, "reverse engineer"—an entire generation of integrated computer circuits. This equipment alone can save the Soviet Union billions of dollars, and significantly reduce the Western lead in microelectronics.[87] In order to be able to steal Western equipment on even a larger scale, the Soviet Union will need the relaxed atmosphere of a new detente—another reason for Gorbachev to launch a new "peace offensive." His options in this regard are virtually countless.

Economic Response

Planning the activities of a huge economy, one which is half the size of the American economy, is obviously a horrendous task. Gosplan, the State Planning Committee, currently plans the production of twenty-five million basic types of products, and the number is constantly growing. Manufacturing this number of basic products requires planning the production and distribution of several billion parts and components. This is impossible even theoretically. As the academician Fedorenko has remarked, "to properly balance, check and correct this kind of plan would take 30,000 years even with the help of computers."[88]

Putting together a five-year plan, to say nothing of a fifteen-year plan, is obviously a task of staggering dimensions. It is an even less possible task when—as is the case—the contribution of the East European economies must be factored in. The East Europeans have mixed feelings about further economic and scientific cooperation and integration with the Soviet Union. On the one hand, they benefit from it in the short run, because their industrial products are not qualitatively competitive on the international markets. On the other hand, growing dependence on Soviet bloc trade inhibits them even more, and widens the technological gap between them and the West. Therefore, persuading them to reconsider their plans, and cut back on cooperation with the West in favor of expanded trade with the Soviet Union, requires considerable political pressure and time.

From the Soviet leadership's viewpoint, it has plenty of room to maneuver within the existing economic system. The Party might revitalize the twenty-year old concept of contract work, and put a substantial number of scientists and engineers to work on a contract basis. The idea would be to compensate them for the actual work done rather than paying them fixed salaries. This way, scientists and engineers can earn four to five times more, and their productivity increases tremendously.

The Party could also lure scientists by offering access to the hard currency shops, paying them partially in special certificates. As Michael Checinski, an analyst from the U.S. Army Russian Research Center, has correctly observed:

[87] *Wall Street Journal*, November 11, 1985.

[88] Quoted in Alec Nove, "Is a Within-System Reform Possible?" presented at the *Geneva Congress of Sovietologists*, August 13-18, 1985.

In a Soviet-style economy, precisely because of the lack of many common products and services, the employer can offer different incentives without increasing the salaries of his workers. Improved housing conditions, faster permission to buy furniture, a better TV set, a car, better food or clothing, a kindergarden, a summer vacation, and the like are valued by workers more than increased salaries and act as a stronger incentive for harder work.[89]

The Party will certainly equip several hundred high schools and colleges with American computers.

The Party might also try to resolve the problem of quality by massive robotization. Existing Soviet plans indicate an intention to increase dramatically the number of robots in Soviet industry. By 1990, the Party plans to have 200,000 robots in socialist bloc countries. In comparison, the United States is expected to have 80,000 robots by 1990. Of course these plans—as is often the case with Soviet economic planning—are not necessarily going to materialize. However, the intention is very revealing. It is not extraordinary for the Soviet Union to purchase entire factories. This time it could purchase fully automated factories made in Japan or West Germany—which would churn out microprocessors by the thousands.

Hungary might be allowed to drift even further toward the West as long as it provides the Soviets with Western expertise, software, and so on. For similar reasons, East Germany might be encouraged to cooperate even more closely with West Germany.

It would be typical for the Party to create a huge new "Ministry of Cosmic Defense," combining different branches from various ministries so that the new ministry had everything it needed to "provide a reliable cosmic defense against the imperialists." In fact, there is a report indicating that this measure has already been taken. *Pravda* reported on October 28, 1985 that the *Glavkosmos*—the Chief Administration for Development and Use of Space Technology for National Economy and Scientific Research—has been established. The Party is obviously laying the groundwork for a long-term technological competition with the "American imperialists."

At the moment, however, it is not yet clear which technologies are going to be chosen by the U.S. scientific and industrial communities as the most efficient and feasible for SDI. Therefore, the Soviet leadership has yet to make its final plans. When these technologies are sufficiently mature, the Party will move very quickly. The Soviets may be the first to apply these technologies, taken off the Western shelf, to their military machine. This has happened several times in the past, and might well happen again if U.S. politics follows its familiar on-again, off-again pattern in military procurement. In this regard, a consistent (even if modest) increase of the U.S. defense budget would be strongly desirable.

[89] Unpublished paper, presented at the *Geneva Conference of Sovietologists*, August 13-18, 1985.

The Party is patient. The Soviet leadership believes that the initial American romance with the idea of a nuclear shield will not last more than five to seven years; that long before then the American people will start questioning the utility and efficiency of such a program, which could well result in its substantial retardation before it even reaches maturity.

Finally, nobody will ever be able to argue convincingly that any BMD system will be one hundred percent impregnable. Therefore, SDI's critics—the Soviets among them—always will have an argument that is impossible to refute. The fact that one hundred percent effectiveness is not a necessary attribute of an effective BMD system does not seem to make any noticeable impact on the minds of the critics. With the Soviets, it is undoubtedly otherwise.

Conclusion

This is not a study of strategy, but the Strategic Defense Initiative is unavoidably a key element of future U.S. strategy. Therefore, some words on what needs to be done in a more general sense are appropriate here.

The Soviet Union's resources are huge, and the Party's potential for maneuvering is immense. But the problems that the Soviet Union faces are immense also. The problem of its own population is the most intractable of them. The people who smile at Gorbachev when he "casually" talks to them in Victory Park in Kiev—who readily say, "Yes, of course, comrade General Secretary"—in their hearts are saying, "We are tired of fighting, particularly for your Party's fat cats and their goals."

At times, the Western press entertains the following notion: Soviet society is corrupt, and comatose; a new, vigorous, reform-minded leader is needed who can single-handedly awaken it, as did Peter the Great and Lenin. Gorbachev emerges in this scenario as a progressive leader who is desperately trying to overcome the resistance and inertia of the bureaucracy. Some Western journalists even go so far as to hint that some sort of nostalgia for the whip allegedly exists among many Russians. There is perhaps nothing more ignorant, arrogant, and stupid than this philosophy; its proponents should be counselled to find simpler objects for their intellectual pursuits than the Soviet Union. The Soviet people are very much alive and active. However, they are sick and tired of struggle. They are physically and emotionally tired. They have to hide their energy and activity from the government, and this is why many foreign journalists do not see it. Their activity is hidden behind their own individual Potemkin village facades. In fact, almost all Soviet people, including a majority of the Party and KGB officials, already sabotage many of the Party's initiatives and plans. This opposition is so invisible, so subtle, so difficult to grasp and deal with, and yet so pervasive, that any Party initiative, campaign or drive will drown in it in two or three months. This was the fate of Gorbachev's antialcohol campaign; the discipline campaign, efficiency campaign, and resource-saving campaign met similar ends.

Widespread terror could perhaps force the people to participate in the Party's struggle more actively. But even if the Party were ready to opt for such a solution, the creativity required by the new technological era cannot flourish under the pressure of fear. Not even Gorbachev has the nerve for Stalin-like measures, although everything he has been doing so far indicates his emphasis on "tightening the screws," albeit with a pleasant smile.

The invisible confrontation between the Party and the people behind the facade of unity is likely to continue and grow. This rift is the West's biggest hope. The people of the Soviet Union are our natural allies—not only the ethnic minorities but, above all, the core of the empire, the Great Russians.

The Soviet empire is a unique entity from many standpoints. One of its most peculiar aspects is that the people who constitute the core of the empire have the lowest living standards and fewest freedoms within the realm. The only opportunities for Great Russians to live in warmer climates—or to enjoy a higher quality of life and a little freedom—are found on the fringes of the empire. The only other way is to make it to the top of the state pyramid—that is, inadvertently to serve the Party.

As with any very highly organized institution, the Party has a very strong instinct for survival. Therefore, we cannot expect it to commit political suicide. However, every individual Party member has his own instinct for survival, which does not necessarily coincide with the Party's instinct. This makes every Party member a potential defector. Thus, the erosion of the Party's political power is not only possible, but feasible, and should be promoted. The Party should be deprived of its material, ideological, and human bases, and for that it should be challenged simultaneously on all fronts: the economic, technological, scientific, ideological, and diplomatic.

It should be made clear to everybody—to the developing nations, Soviet client states, the Soviet population, and Party members themselves—that the Party is not the brain and nervous system, neither of the nation nor of mankind. Instead, it consists of ordinary human beings, who have been the first victims of the stifling Party structure.

In order to prevent the achievement of patchwork solutions—stealing or buying Western technologies, maneuvering and recruiting new naively idealistic people, creating new troubles in the world, and so on—this challenge must be comprehensive, decisive, and obvious. We should keep in mind the example of China, which embarked on a venture of reforms only after three decade-long attempts to modernize the nation had failed.

The Communist Party of the USSR should forget its ambitions of ruling the world, should recognize the right of the capitalist system to exist, should renounce its role as the vanguard of mankind, and should liberate mankind from its tutelage. It is the Party, not mankind, who should and must be reeducated. A technological defeat by itself obviously cannot achieve all these results, but it would be an essential element in the overall defeat of the Party. SDI could be a vehicle for such a defeat.

Finally, assuming that some BMD technologies have reached reasonable maturity, we would benefit by partially adopting the Soviet attitude toward weapons procurement and beginning the deployment of even a marginally effective missile defense system as soon as possible. The deployment of even a 10 percent effective BMD system would be advisable for several reasons. First, it would endlessly complicate Soviet military plans and greatly reduce both the probability of a Soviet first nuclear strike and their ability to exploit politically the threat of such a strike. Second, it would demonstrate the seriousness of the U.S. intention to do away with the nuclear threat. It would demolish speculation about the technical impossibility of missile defense, and make possible a the gradual reduction of offensive weapons in the not so remote future, thus bringing about a reduction of costs. Third, the gradual improvement of the system by the introduction of new layers of defense would be the least damaging politically. This would give SDI a life of its own, and bring needed consistency to U.S. foreign policy through the rest of the century. Finally, early deployment of BMD by the United States would compel the Soviet Union leadership to take immediate and strategically important decisions concerning the development of certain sectors of their economy, military technology, and science—thus giving new momentum to advocates of market reform in the Soviet leadership.

We are moving into a new technological era. The Party, with its antiquated perceptions of the world and ridiculous imperial ambitions, should be left behind where it belongs. If, on the other hand, it is capable of changing its thinking, we should stimulate its efforts toward developing computers, the basic infrastructure, and the quality of life for the Soviet population. Without the ability to compete in these fundamental areas, the Party will eventually be forced to drop out of the power race with which it is now obsessed.

We can win the hearts of the Party's reluctant soldiers, particularly those of young people. We can bring to them a message of hope in place of the despondency with which they now live, a message of love and cooperation instead of hatred and struggle.

We can also bring hope to those young Americans who believe that nuclear war is inevitable and could very well happen during their lifetime. How can one possibly build a meaningful life with such a fear in his heart?

PERGAMON-BRASSEY'S
International Defense Publishers

List of Publications
published for the
Institute for Foreign Policy Analysis, Inc.

Orders for the following titles should be addressed to: Pergamon-Brassey's, Maxwell House, Fairview Park, Elmsford, New York, 10523; or to Pergamon-Brassey's, Headington Hill Hall, Oxford, OX3 0BW, England.

Foreign Policy Reports

ETHICS, DETERRENCE, AND NATIONAL SECURITY. By James E. Dougherty, Midge Decter, Pierre Hassner, Laurence Martin, Michael Novak, and Vladimir Bukovsky. 1985. xvi, 91pp. $9.95.

AMERICAN SEA POWER AND GLOBAL STRATEGY. By Robert J. Hanks. 1985. viii, 92pp. $9.95.

DECISION-MAKING IN COMMUNIST COUNTRIES: AN INSIDE VIEW. By Jan Sejna and Joseph D. Douglass, Jr. 1986. xii, 75pp. $9.95.

NATIONAL SECURITY: ETHICS, STRATEGY, AND POLITICS. A LAYMAN'S PRIMER. By Robert L. Pfaltzgraff, Jr. 1986. v, 37pp. $9.95.

DETERRING CHEMICAL WARFARE: U.S. POLICY OPTIONS FOR THE 1990S. By Hugh Stringer. 1986. xii, 71pp. $9.95.

THE CRISIS OF COMMUNISM: ITS MEANING, ORIGINS, AND PHASES. By Rett R. Ludwikowski. 1986. xii, 79pp. $9.95.

TRANSATLANTIC DISCORD AND NATO'S CRISIS OF COHESION. By Peter H. Langer. 1986. viii, 89pp. $9.95.

THE REORGANIZATION OF THE JOINT CHIEFS OF STAFF: A CRITICAL ANALYSIS. Contributions by Allan R. Millett, Mackubin Thomas Owens, Bernard E. Trainor, Edward C. Meyer, and Robert Murray. 1986. xi, 67pp. $9.95.

Special Reports

STRATEGIC MINERALS AND INTERNATIONAL SECURITY. Edited by Uri Ra'anan and Charles M. Perry. 1985. viii, 85pp. $9.95.

THIRD WORLD MARXIST-LENINIST REGIMES: STRENGTHS, VULNERABILITIES, AND U.S. POLICY. By Uri Ra'anan, Francis Fukuyama, Mark Falcoff, Sam C. Sarkesian, and Richard H. Shultz, Jr. 1985. xv, 125pp. $9.95.

THE RED ARMY ON PAKISTAN'S BORDER: POLICY IMPLICATIONS FOR THE UNITED STATES. By Anthony Arnold, Richard P. Cronin, Thomas Perry Thornton, Theodore L. Eliot, Jr., and Robert L. Pfaltzgraff, Jr. 1986. vi, 83pp. $9.95.

ASYMMETRIES IN U.S. AND SOVIET STRATEGIC DEFENSE PROGRAMS: IMPLICATIONS FOR NEAR-TERM AMERICAN DEPLOYMENT OPTIONS. By William A. Davis, Jr. 1986. xi, 71pp. $9.95.

REGIONAL SECURITY AND ANTI-TACTICAL BALLISTIC MISSILES: POLITICAL AND TECHNICAL ISSUES. By William A. Davis, Jr. 1986. xii, 54pp. $9.95.

NAVAL FORCES AND WESTERN SECURITY. By Francis J. West, Jr., Jacquelyn K. Davis, James E. Dougherty, Robert J. Hanks, and Charles M. Perry. 1987. xi, 55pp, Tables. $9.95.

Books

ATLANTIC COMMUNITY IN CRISIS: A REDEFINITION OF THE ATLANTIC RELATIONSHIP. Edited by Walter F. Hahn and Robert L. Pfaltzgraff, Jr. 1979. 386pp. $43.00.

REVISING U.S. MILITARY STRATEGY: TAILORING MEANS TO ENDS. By Jeffrey Record. 1984. 113pp. $16.95 ($9.95, paper).

SHATTERING EUROPE'S DEFENSE CONSENSUS: THE ANTINUCLEAR PROTEST MOVEMENT AND THE FUTURE OF NATO. Edited by James E. Dougherty and Robert L. Pfaltzgraff, Jr. 1985. 226pp. $18.95.

INSTITUTE FOR FOREIGN POLICY ANALYSIS, INC.
List of Publications

Orders for the following titles in IFPA's series of Special Reports, Foreign Policy Reports, National Security Papers, Conference Reports, and Books should be addressed to the Circulation Manager, Institute for Foreign Policy Analysis, Central Plaza Building, Tenth Floor, 675 Massachusetts Avenue, Cambridge, Massachusetts 02139-3396. (Telephone: 617-492-2116.) Please send a check or money order for the correct amount together with your order.

Foreign Policy Reports

DEFENSE TECHNOLOGY AND THE ATLANTIC ALLIANCE: COMPETITION OR COLLABORATION? By Frank T.J. Bray and Michael Moodie. April 1977. vi, 42pp. $5.00.

IRAN'S QUEST FOR SECURITY: U.S. ARMS TRANSFERS AND THE NUCLEAR OPTION. By Alvin J. Cottrell and James E. Dougherty. May 1977. 59pp. $5.00.

ETHIOPIA, THE HORN OF AFRICA, AND U.S. POLICY. By John H. Spencer. September 1977. 69pp. $5.00.

BEYOND THE ARAB-ISRAELI SETTLEMENT: NEW DIRECTIONS FOR U.S. POLICY IN THE MIDDLE EAST. By R.K. Ramazani. September 1977. viii, 69pp. $5.00.

SPAIN, THE MONARCHY AND THE ATLANTIC COMMUNITY. By David C. Jordan. June 1979. v, 55pp. $5.00.

U.S. STRATEGY AT THE CROSSROADS: TWO VIEWS. By Robert J. Hanks and Jeffrey Record. July 1982. viii, 69pp. $7.50.

THE U.S. MILITARY PRESENCE IN THE MIDDLE EAST: PROBLEMS AND PROSPECTS. By Robert J. Hanks. December 1982. vii, 77pp. $7.50.

SOUTHERN AFRICA AND WESTERN SECURITY. By Robert J. Hanks. August 1983. vii, 71pp. $7.50.

THE WEST GERMAN PEACE MOVEMENT AND THE NATIONAL QUESTION. By Kim R. Holmes. March 1984. x, 73pp. $7.50.

THE HISTORY AND IMPACT OF MARXIST-LENINIST ORGANIZATIONAL THEORY. By John P. Roche. April 1984. x, 70pp. $7.50.

Special Reports

THE CRUISE MISSILE: BARGAINING CHIP OR DEFENSE BARGAIN? By Robert L. Pfaltzgraff, Jr., and Jacquelyn K. Davis. January 1977. x, 53pp. $3.00.

EUROCOMMUNISM AND THE ATLANTIC ALLIANCE. By James E. Dougherty and Diane K. Pfaltzgraff. January 1977. xiv, 66pp. $3.00.

THE NEUTRON BOMB: POLITICAL, TECHNICAL, AND MILITARY ISSUES. By S.T. Cohen. November 1978. xii, 95pp. $6.50.

SALT II AND U.S.-SOVIET STRATEGIC FORCES. By Jacquelyn K. Davis, Patrick J. Friel, and Robert L. Pfaltzgraff, Jr. June 1979. xii, 51pp. $5.00.

THE EMERGING STRATEGIC ENVIRONMENT: IMPLICATIONS FOR BALLISTIC MISSILE DEFENSE. By Leon Gouré, William G. Hyland, and Colin S. Gray. December 1979. xi, 75pp. $6.50.

THE SOVIET UNION AND BALLISTIC MISSILE DEFENSE. By Jacquelyn K. Davis, Uri Ra'anan, Robert L. Pfaltzgraff, Jr., Michael J. Deane, and John M. Collins. March 1980. xi, 71pp. $6.50. (Out of print).

ENERGY ISSUES AND ALLIANCE RELATIONSHIPS: THE UNITED STATES, WESTERN EUROPE AND JAPAN. By Robert L. Pfaltzgraff, Jr. April 1980. xii, 71pp. $6.50.

U.S. STRATEGIC-NUCLEAR POLICY AND BALLISTIC MISSILE DEFENSE: THE 1980S AND BEYOND. By William Schneider, Jr., Donald G. Brennan, William A. Davis, Jr., and Hans Rühle. April 1980. xii, 61pp. $6.50.

THE UNNOTICED CHALLENGE: SOVIET MARITIME STRATEGY AND THE GLOBAL CHOKE POINTS. By Robert J. Hanks. August 1980. xi, 66pp. $6.50.

FORCE REDUCTIONS IN EUROPE: STARTING OVER. By Jeffrey Record. October 1980. xi, 91pp. $6.50.

SALT II AND AMERICAN SECURITY. By Gordon J. Humphrey, William R. Van Cleave, Jeffrey Record, William H. Kincade, and Richard Perle. October 1980. xvi, 65pp.

THE FUTURE OF U.S. LAND-BASED STRATEGIC FORCES. By Jake Garn, J.I. Coffey, Lord Chalfont, and Ellery B. Block. December 1980. xvi, 80pp.

THE CAPE ROUTE: IMPERILED WESTERN LIFELINE. By Robert J. Hanks. February 1981. xi, 80pp. $6.50. (Hardcover, $10.00).

POWER PROJECTION AND THE LONG-RANGE COMBAT AIRCRAFT: MISSIONS, CAPABILITIES AND ALTERNATIVE DESIGNS. By Jacquelyn K. Davis and Robert L. Pfaltzgraff, Jr. June 1981. ix, 37pp. $6.50.

THE PACIFIC FAR EAST: ENDANGERED AMERICAN STRATEGIC POSITION. By Robert J. Hanks. October 1981. vii, 75pp. $7.50.

NATO'S THEATER NUCLEAR FORCE MODERNIZATION PROGRAM: THE REAL ISSUES. By Jeffrey Record. November 1981. viii, 102pp. $7.50.

THE CHEMISTRY OF DEFEAT: ASYMMETRIES IN U.S. AND SOVIET CHEMICAL WARFARE POSTURES. By Amoretta M. Hoeber. December 1981. xiii, 91pp. $6.50.

THE HORN OF AFRICA: A MAP OF POLITICAL-STRATEGIC CONFLICT. By James E. Dougherty. April 1982. xv, 74pp. $7.50.

THE WEST, JAPAN AND CAPE ROUTE IMPORTS: THE OIL AND NON-FUEL MINERAL TRADES. By Charles Perry. June 1982. xiv, 88pp. $7.50.

THE RAPID DEPLOYMENT FORCE AND U.S. MILITARY INTERVENTION IN THE PERSIAN GULF. By Jeffrey Record. May 1983, Second Edition. viii, 83pp. $7.50.

THE GREENS OF WEST GERMANY: ORIGINS, STRATEGIES, AND TRANSATLANTIC IMPLICATIONS. By Robert L. Pfaltzgraff, Jr., Kim R. Holmes, Clay Clemens, and Werner Kaltefleiter. August 1983. xi, 105pp. $7.50.

THE ATLANTIC ALLIANCE AND U.S. GLOBAL STRATEGY. By Jacquelyn K. Davis and Robert L. Pfaltzgraff, Jr. September 1983. x, 44pp. $7.50.

WORLD ENERGY SUPPLY AND INTERNATIONAL SECURITY. By Herman Franssen, John P. Hardt, Jacquelyn K. Davis, Robert J. Hanks, Charles Perry, Robert L. Pfaltzgraff, Jr., and Jeffrey Record. October 1983. xiv, 93pp. $7.50.

POISONING ARMS CONTROL: THE SOVIET UNION AND CHEMICAL/BIOLOGICAL WEAPONS. By Mark C. Storella. June 1984. xi, 99pp. $7.50.

National Security Papers

CBW: THE POOR MAN'S ATOMIC BOMB. By Neil C. Livingstone and Joseph D. Douglass, Jr., with a Foreword by Senator John Tower. February 1984. x, 33pp. $5.00.

U.S. STRATEGIC AIRLIFT: REQUIREMENTS AND CAPABILITIES. By Jeffrey Record. January 1986. vi, 38pp. $6.00.

STRATEGIC BOMBERS: HOW MANY ARE ENOUGH? By Jeffrey Record. January 1986. vi, 22pp. $6.00.

STRATEGIC DEFENSE AND EXTENDED DETERRENCE: A NEW TRANSATLANTIC DEBATE. By Jacquelyn K. Davis and Robert L. Pfaltzgraff, Jr. February 1986. viii, 51pp. $8.00.

JCS REORGANIZATION AND U.S. ARMS CONTROL POLICY. By James E. Dougherty. March 1986. xiv, 27pp. $6.00.

STRATEGIC FORCE MODERNIZATION AND ARMS CONTROL. Contributions by Edward L. Rowny, R. James Woolsey, Harold Brown, Alexander M. Haig, Jr., Albert Gore, Jr., Brent Scowcroft, Russell E. Dougherty, A. Casey, Gordon Fornell, and Sam Nunn. 1986. xiii, 43pp. $6.00.

U.S. BOMBER FORCE MODERNIZATION. Contributions by Mike Synar, Richard K. Betts, William Kaufmann, Russell E. Dougherty, Richard DeLauer, and Dan Quayle. 1986. vii, 9pp. $5.00.

U.S. STRATEGIC AIRLIFT CHOICES. Contributions by William S. Cohen, Russell Murray, Frederick G. Kroesen, William Kaufmann, Harold Brown, James A. Courter, and Robert W. Komer. 1986. ix, 13pp. $5.00.

Books

SOVIET MILITARY STRATEGY IN EUROPE. By Joseph D. Douglass, Jr. Pergamon Press, 1980. 252pp. (Out of print).

THE WARSAW PACT: ARMS, DOCTRINE, AND STRATEGY. By William J. Lewis. New York: McGraw-Hill Publishing Co., 1982. 471pp. $15.00.

THE BISHOPS AND NUCLEAR WEAPONS: THE CATHOLIC PASTORAL LETTER ON WAR AND PEACE. By James E. Dougherty. Archon Books, 1984. 255pp. $22.50.

Conference Reports

NATO AND ITS FUTURE: A GERMAN-AMERICAN ROUNDTABLE. Summary of a Dialogue. 1978. 22pp. $1.00.

SECOND GERMAN-AMERICAN ROUNDTABLE ON NATO: THE THEATER-NUCLEAR BALANCE. 1978. 32pp. $1.00.

THE SOVIET UNION AND BALLISTIC MISSILE DEFENSE. 1978. 26pp. $1.00.

U.S. STRATEGIC-NUCLEAR POLICY AND BALLISTIC MISSILE DEFENSE: THE 1980S AND BEYOND. 1979. 30pp. $1.00.

SALT II AND AMERICAN SECURITY. 1979. 39pp.

THE FUTURE OF U.S. LAND-BASED STRATEGIC FORCES. 1979. 32pp.

THE FUTURE OF NUCLEAR POWER. 1980. 48pp. $1.00.

THIRD GERMAN-AMERICAN ROUNDTABLE ON NATO: MUTUAL AND BALANCED FORCE REDUCTIONS IN EUROPE. 1980. 27pp. $1.00.

FOURTH GERMAN-AMERICAN ROUNDTABLE ON NATO: NATO MODERNIZATION AND EUROPEAN SECURITY. 1981. 15pp. $1.00.

SECOND ANGLO-AMERICAN SYMPOSIUM ON DETERRENCE AND EUROPEAN SECURITY. 1981. 25pp. $1.00.

The U.S. Defense Mobilization Infrastructure: Problems and Priorities. The Tenth Annual Conference, sponsored by the International Security Studies Program, The Fletcher School of Law and Diplomacy, Tufts University. 1981. 25pp. $1.00.

U.S. Strategic Doctrine for the 1980s. 1982. 14pp.

French-American Symposium on Strategy, Deterrence and European Security. 1982. 14pp. $1.00.

Fifth German-American Roundtable on NATO: The Changing Context of the European Security Debate. Summary of a Transatlantic Dialogue. 1982. 22pp. $1.00.

Energy Security and the Future of Nuclear Power. 1982. 39pp. $2.50.

International Security Dimensions of Space. The Eleventh Annual Conference, sponsored by the International Security Studies Program, The Fletcher School of Law and Diplomacy, Tufts University. 1982. 24pp. $2.50.

Portugal, Spain and Transatlantic Relations. Summary of a Transatlantic Dialogue. 1983. 18pp. $2.50.

Japanese-American Symposium on Reducing Strategic Minerals Vulnerabilities: Current Plans, Priorities, and Possibilities for Cooperation. 1983. 31pp. $2.50.

National Security Policy: The Decision-Making Process. The Twelfth Annual Conference, sponsored by the International Security Studies Program, The Fletcher School of Law and Diplomacy, Tufts University. 1983. 28pp. $2.50.

The Security of the Atlantic, Iberian and North African Regions. Summary of a Transatlantic Dialogue. 1983. 25pp. $2.50.

The West European Antinuclear Protest Movement: Implications for Western Security. Summary of a Transatlantic Dialogue. 1984. 21pp. $2.50.

The U.S.-Japanese Security Relationship in Transition. Summary of a Transpacific Dialogue. 1984. 23pp. $2.50.

Sixth German-American Roundtable on NATO: NATO and European Security—Beyond INF. Summary of a Transatlantic Dialogue. 1984. 31pp. $2.50.

Security Commitments and Capabilities: Elements of an American Global Strategy. The Thirteenth Annual Conference, sponsored by the International Security Studies Program, The Fletcher School of Law and Diplomacy, Tufts University. 1984. 21pp. $2.50.

Third Japanese-American-German Conference on the Future of Nuclear Energy. 1984. 40pp. $2.50.

Seventh German-American Roundtable on NATO: Political Constraints, Emerging Technologies, and Alliance Strategy. Summary of a Transatlantic Dialogue. 1985. 36pp. $2.50.

Terrorism and Other "Low-Intensity" Operations: International Linkages. The Fourteenth Annual Conference, sponsored by the International Security Studies Program, The Fletcher School of Law and Diplomacy, Tufts University. 1985. 21pp. $2.50.

East-West Trade and Technology Transfer: New Challenges for the United States. Second Annual Forum, co-sponsored by the Institute for Foreign Policy Analysis and the International Security Studies Program, The Fletcher School of Law and Diplomacy, Tufts University. 1986. 40pp. $3.50.

Organizing for National Security: The Role of the Joint Chiefs of Staff. 1986. 32pp. $2.50.

Eighth German-American Roundtable on NATO: Strategic Defense, NATO Modernization, and East-West Relations. Summary of a Transatlantic Dialogue. 1986. 47pp. $2.50.

Emerging Doctrines and Technologies: Implications for Global and Regional Political-Military Balances. The Fifteenth Annual Conference, sponsored by the International

Security Studies Program, The Fletcher School of Law and Diplomacy, Tufts University. 1986. 49pp. $2.50.

STRATEGIC WAR TERMINATION: POLITICAL-MILITARY-DIPLOMATIC DIMENSIONS. 1986. 22pp. $2.50.

SDI AND EUROPEAN SECURITY: ENHANCING CONVENTIONAL DEFENSE. 21 pp. $2.50.